EAU CLAIRE DISTRICT LIBRARY
6528 East Main Street
P.O. Box 328
EAU CLAIRE, MI 49111

J
362.29
Med

W9-AXA-936

Medical Marijuana

Titles in the Issues That Concern You series include:

ISSUES THAT CONCERN YOU

Medical Marijuana

Elaine Minamide, *Book Editor*

Chris Nasso, *Publisher*
Elizabeth Des Chenes, *Managing Editor*

GREENHAVEN PRESS
A part of Gale, Cengage Learning

EAU CLAIRE DISTRICT LIBRARY

GALE
CENGAGE Learning™

Detroit • New York • San Francisco • New Haven, Conn • Waterville, Maine • London

T 144491

© 2007 Gale, Cengage Learning

For more information, contact
Greenhaven Press
27500 Drake Rd.
Farmington Hills, MI 48331-3535
Or you can visit our Internet site at gale.cengage.com

ALL RIGHTS RESERVED.
No part of this work covered by the copyright hereon may be reproduced or used in any form or by any means—graphic, electronic, or mechanical, including photocopying, recording, taping, Web distribution or information storage retrieval systems—without the written permission of the publisher.

Articles in Greenhaven Press anthologies are often edited for length to meet page requirements. In addition, original titles of these works are changed to clearly present the main thesis and to explicitly indicate the author's opinion. Every effort is made to ensure that Greenhaven Press accurately reflects the original intent of the authors.

Every effort has been made to trace the owners of copyrighted material.

LIBRARY OF CONGRESS CATALOGING-IN-PUBLICATION DATA

Medical marijuana / Elaine Minamide, book editor.
       p. cm. — (Issues that concern you)
Includes bibliographical references and index.
ISBN 0-7377-3495-7 (hardcover : alk. paper)
1. Marijuana—Therapeutic use--United States. 2. Marijuana—Law and legislation—United States. 3. Drug legalization—United States. I. Minamide, Elaine.
RM666.C266M43 2007
362.29'5—dc22

                                           2006026978

Printed in the United States of America
5 6 7 12 11 10 09 08

CONTENTS

Many medicines legally used today can trace their pharmacological history to folk medicine and herbal remedies. Drugs like aspirin (derived from willow bark), digitalis (foxglove), quinine (cinchona), and morphine (opium poppy) are all plant-based drugs whose herbal forms have been around for centuries.

Like these and other drugs, marijuana (*Cannabis sativa*), is a naturally occurring substance, an ordinary weed growing wild in many parts of the world. And also like some of these drugs, marijuana has a long history in U.S. pharmacology. According to Mitch Earleywine, author of *Understanding Marijuana: A New Look at the Scientific Evidence*, "Medicinal use of cannabis began around 2737 B.C.," and historical documentation of its use can be traced to ancient China, Egypt, and India as well as ancient Rome and Greece. In American history, references to marijuana prescriptions turn up as early as 1764. It was not until 1941 that marijuana was removed from the *U.S. Pharmacopoeia*, the list of officially sanctioned medicines.

Marijuana's path to disrepute culminated in the early 1970s, after Congress passed the Controlled Substances Act (CSA). The CSA sorts drugs into five classifications, or schedules, and dictates what drugs doctors are and are not allowed to prescribe. According to the Drug Enforcement Administration (DEA) Web site, drugs are placed in a schedule "based upon the substance's medicinal value, harmfulness, and potential for abuse or addiction." Schedule I drugs are reserved for "the most dangerous drugs that have no recognized medical use," while Schedule V drugs are the least dangerous drugs. Marijuana was categorized as a Schedule I drug, which, according to the CSA, means that it has "a high potential for abuse, no currently accepted medical use in treatment in the United States, and a lack of accepted safety for use of the drug or other substance under medical supervision." Other Schedule I drugs include heroin and lysergic acid diethylamide

(LSD). Schedule II drugs, which are considered highly dangerous but can be used as medicine, include cocaine, morphine, and opium.

Since the 1970s marijuana has remained illegal in the United States. However, within the last decade or so, its medical potential has been reexamined. Claims that marijuana provides relief for a variety of ailments, including symptoms related to AIDS, glaucoma, spasticity, chronic pain, nausea, and other ailments of the chronically ill, led to well-funded and highly publicized grassroots efforts to destigmatize its use. These efforts resulted in a series of statewide initiatives to legalize medical marijuana. Since 1996, eleven states (Alaska, Arizona, California, Colorado, Hawaii, Maine, Nevada, Oregon, Rhode Island, Vermont, and Washington) have passed laws legalizing medical marijuana for qualifying patients.

However, these laws have placed states—and, consequently, individuals who reside in those states—on a collision course with the federal government, which so far has refused even to consider rescheduling cannabis to a Schedule II drug, which would permit its use in medical treatment under certain circumstances. The ramifications of this conflict are clear. For instance, a patient in a state where medical marijuana is legal might obtain a prescription from a physician to use marijuana for a specific health condition; however, because federal law prohibits the writing of such prescriptions, both the physician and the patient would then be at risk of arrest for doing what is legal in their own state.

Some states have attempted to circumvent such conflicts with the federal government by creating laws that provide some immunity to users of medical marijuana. In 1996, for example, Californians approved a law that required qualifying patients to obtain a "recommendation" (not a prescription) for medical marijuana. By 1998 seven other states had emulated this approach. Though these laws do not provide total immunity from arrest or prosecution, they do offer a haven of sorts to individual users. Even former DEA administrator Asa Hutchinson admitted as much when he was quoted in the *Oakland* (CA) *Tribune* in 2002 as saying, "The federal government is not prosecuting marijuana

Cannabis sativa, *the scientific name for marijuana, has been used medicinally for thousands of years.*

users." In 2004 the Marijuana Policy Project, a nonprofit organization that works to minimize the harm associated with marijuana, published a state-by-state report pointing out that "federal drug agents simply do not have the resources or the mandate to patrol the streets of a state to look for cancer patients growing a few marijuana plants."

The growing acceptance of marijuana as an alternative medicine and the subsequent grassroots efforts to legalize it have troubled many who are on the front lines of the federal government's ongoing war on drugs. Critics oppose efforts to legalize medical marijuana for a variety of reasons. Some argue that less dangerous medicines are available to ease the pain or discomfort of patients. A policy statement on the California Narcotics Officers Association Web site points out that marijuana is "an unstable mixture of over 400 [toxic psychoactive] chemicals." Others maintain that because marijuana is usually inhaled to achieve its supposed benefits, it poses serious health consequences to the user. Many opponents fear that legalizing medical marijuana will undermine the federal government's antidrug efforts by encouraging increased drug use, especially among adolescents. Andrea Barthwell, deputy director of the White House Office of National Drug Control Policy, has stated that "children entering drug abuse treatment programs routinely report that they heard that 'pot is medicine' and, therefore, believed it to be good for them."

Activists demonstrate outside a government building for legal medical use of cannabis.

The potential social consequences of legalizing marijuana for medical purposes is among the topics considered in this anthology. In excerpts from magazine articles, newspaper editorials, and other sources, authors debate the medical benefits of marijuana and how this drug should be regulated by the government. In addition, the volume contains several appendixes to help the reader understand and explore the topic, including a thorough bibliography and a list of organizations to contact for further information. The appendix titled "What You Should Know About Medical Marijuana" offers crucial facts about marijuana and its impact on young people. The appendix "What You Should Do About Medical Marijuana" offers tips to young people who may confront the issue in their own lives. With all these features, *Issues That Concern You: Medical Marijuana* provides an excellent resource for everyone interested in this timely issue.

ONE

Marijuana Is an Effective Medical Treatment

Debra J. Saunders

In the following selection Debra J. Saunders argues that marijuana can help many seriously ill patients and that its use for medical purposes should be legalized. Even though voters in eleven states have approved medical marijuana use by those whose doctors feel its use is justified, the Supreme Court has ruled against them, Saunders writes. The issue must now return to Congress, where lawmakers should consider changing marijuana from its current classification as a Schedule I drug, a category that includes more dangerous drugs like heroin, to a Schedule II drug, like cocaine and morphine, which are available for medical use. This reclassification would give physicians the right to prescribe marijuana to patients whose medical conditions warrant such treatment. Saunders is a syndicated columnist who writes for the *San Francisco Chronicle* and has also written for the *Wall Street Journal*, the *National Review*, the *Weekly Standard*, *Reader's Digest*, and *Reason* magazine.

Someday, Washington will catch up with the 72 percent of Americans over 45 who, according to a 2004 poll by the AARP [American Association for Retired Persons], believe adults should

Debra J. Saunders, "Hard on Drugs, Soft on Suffering," *San Francisco Chronicle*, June 9, 2005. Republished with permission of *San Francisco Chronicle*, conveyed through Copyright Clearance Center, Inc.

be able to use medical marijuana if a physician recommends it. First, however, voters are going to have to make some noise.

Or as Justice John Paul Stevens wrote in [the June 6, 2005,] Supreme Court ruling that upheld the federal government's authority to prosecute medical-marijuana users, despite California's and 10 other states' medical-marijuana laws, "the voices of voters allied with these respondents may one day be heard in the halls of Congress."

Too bad the drug-war hawks have Washington spooked. Lawmakers don't want to appear soft on drugs, so they are afraid to call an end to prosecuting people in pain.

That's why marijuana is a "Schedule I" drug in the federal lexicon, which puts the drug in the same legal classification as heroin. Less dangerous drugs—like cocaine and morphine—fall under Schedule II and are available for medical use. But not marijuana.

That's because there is no recognized medical use for marijuana according to the American Medical Association, the drug warriors respond.

Jimmy Margulies, The Record (Hackensack, NJ), King features Syndicate. Reproduced by permission.

EAU CLAIRE DISTRICT LIBRARY

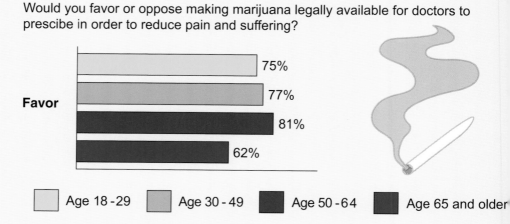

Public Opinion About Marijuana Legalization

Would you favor or oppose making marijuana legally available for doctors to prescibe in order to reduce pain and suffering?

Favor

- 75%
- 77%
- 81%
- 62%

Age 18 -29   Age 30 - 49   Age 50 -64   Age 65 and older

Source: Gallup Organization. Marijuana legalization survey: 2001. Medical marijuana survey: 2003.

Doctors and Patients Have Spoken

Fair enough. But the California Medical Association supports medical marijuana. Chief executive Jack Lewin, a physician, explained that his group believes the government should listen to doctors who recommend the drug. What's more, in passing Proposition 215 in 1996, state voters have spoken, and from what Lewin has seen, "it's not doing a whole lot of harm."

Many California doctors recommend the drug because they've seen salutary results with marijuana not found with its legal pill-form equivalent, Marinol. For some reason, Marinol doesn't take with many patients, who find relief by smoking, drinking or eating marijuana. Marijuana, they say, relieves their nausea, mitigates the ravages of some diseases and increases appetites depressed by chemotherapy.

Doctors have risked their careers recommending an illegal drug. They don't need a study when they can look at the faces of afflicted people who finally have found something that works for them. And many users note that medical marijuana relieves their nausea without drugging them into oblivion.

Sure, some medical-marijuana boosters may be looking for an excuse to smoke pot. Two years ago, I went to a Santa Cruz event where a young man told me he took medical marijuana for an injured knee. Yeah, right.

At the same event, however, I saw a 93-year-old Dorothy Gibbs who suffered from post-polio syndrome. She found that marijuana eased her severe nausea. As a member of the Wo/Men's Alliance for Medical Marijuana [WAMM], Gibbs joined a different lawsuit against federal prosecutions, after the Drug Enforcement Administration raided WAMM and seized 167 marijuana plants.

Gibbs is now dead, WAMM founder Valerie Corral told me on the phone yesterday. In the six months after the raid, 13 WAMM members died—almost 10 percent of WAMM's members. This is a group of seriously ill people—and the kid with the bad knee was not one of them.

Corral, an epileptic, believes she suffers fewer seizures because of medical marijuana. She used to take more powerful pharmaceutical drugs that "made me feel as if I was underwater." With marijuana, she said, she is more functional.

Time for Congress to Act

Back to Congress. Ten states have legalized medical marijuana. Republicans who believe in states' rights should support these states, but in 2004, only 19 Republicans voted for a measure by Rep. Dana Rohrabacher, R- Huntington Beach (Orange County), that would have blocked federal enforcement for users of medical marijuana in states that have legalized its use. It failed 268 to 148.

Rep. Bill Thomas, R-Bakersfield, voted for such a measure in 2003, but backed off in 2004. [In the San Francisco area], Rep. Richard Pombo, R-Tracy, voted "no" [in 2004].

"We've got 70 percent of the Democrats," said Bill Piper, of the anti-drug-war Drug Policy Alliance. Most, but not all. Rep. Dennis Cardoza, D- Modesto, is one of two California House Democrats, as Piper put it, "voting against their own state."

I got no answer from the staff of Pombo or Cardoza as to how either of them plan to vote on [the] Hinchey-Rohrabacher bill, [which would reschedule marijuana so that physicians could legally prescribe it]. Which means, perhaps, they could be swayed by input from constituents.

The White House drug czar John Walters has been a strong opponent of medical marijuana. As he sees it, potheads are using sick people to push marijuana.

I am sure he is right. And I don't care. This year I watched a friend die who lived longer, I believe, because she could drink a tea that revived her appetite, mitigated her need for other pain control and probably bought her a few extra weeks with her children. Marinol didn't help her. Marijuana did.

So I'll quote what Dr. Marcus Conant once said to me. Conant is the doctor who identified the first cases of Kaposi's sarcoma among San Francisco AIDS patients. He also successfully sued to stop the federal government from acting against doctors who recommend medical marijuana.

Conant explained: "To deny sick people relief because of abuse is not humane."

TWO

Marijuana Is Not an Effective Medical Treatment

Sandra Bennett and William Bennett

> Medical marijuana advocates contend that legalizing marijuana for medical purposes is an act of compassion toward the sick and dying. In the following selection Sandra Bennett and William Bennett argue that this message of compassion is misleading and that marijuana is neither safe nor effective. Better drugs are available for all the conditions medical marijuana is supposed to help, the authors insist, and the attempt to legalize marijuana by means of voter referenda bypasses the safeguards established by the federal government to protect the public from harmful drugs. Sandra Bennett is executive director of the Northwest Center for Health and Safety, an organization that makes information on health-related issues supported by scientific research available to the public. William Bennett, former secretary of education, is the medical director at Solid Organ and Cellular Transplantation at Legacy Good Samaritan Hospital and is a retired professor of medicine at Oregon Health Sciences University. He was also the cochairman of Partnership for a Drug-Free America.

Since the early 1970s, there have been repeated attempts to legalize marijuana cigarettes for personal recreational use. In

Sandra Bennett and William Bennett, "Pro-Drug Advocates Market Marijuana to State Legislatures: 'Medical' Marijuana Is a Hoax!" *Drug Watch World News*, vol. VII, October 8, 2003. Reproduced by permission of the authors.

the 1970s and 1980s, these efforts, typically staged by counter-culture organizations, were poorly funded, poorly organized, and met repeated failure.

In the late 1970s, the drug culture began an attempt to gain acceptance of marijuana by clothing it in the wraps of legitimacy, calling it "medical" marijuana. In 1991, at a conference of the National Organization of Marijuana Laws (NORML), Eric Sterling, an outspoken advocate for legalizing marijuana and other drugs, told the audience that they would have to change the politics of the people. "Packaging is important and messages get packaged!" He told them, ". . . we're talking about medical marijuana, which I think our key focus issue ought to be."

Sterling's words were given impetus in 1994 when international entrepreneur and billionaire George Soros advised the Drug Policy Foundation (DPF), a "drug policy reform" group formed in 1986 to give the pro-legalization effort a "more professional look," that he would fund their efforts if they would ". . . target a few winnable issues like medical marijuana. . . ."

Successful Media Campaign

Drug legalizers heeded Soros's advice and in 1996 orchestrated the ballot initiative in California (Proposition 215) to allow Californians with certain medical conditions to grow and smoke marijuana as medicine. The successful passage of Proposition 215 typified how successfully a well-funded media campaign, regardless of the message, can win acceptance. This is particularly so when the message is packaged as an appeal to the human capacity for caring and compassion. The successful advertising campaign responsible for the passage of Prop 215 was made possible by a tremendous influx of out-of-state money from George Soros and his wealthy cohorts, [billionaires] Peter Lewis and John Sperling. Voters were deluged with misleading media messages of compassion for the sick and dying, and they responded by approving the smoking of marijuana cigarettes as "medicine."

After the success in California, legalizers, using this same strategy, took their message to several other states that had initiative

This marijuana, chopped and ready for use, was grown by the federal government for research.

procedures, and they were successful in effecting passage of "medical" marijuana cigarette initiatives in an additional eight states.

Proponents of legalization next targeted state legislatures and succeeded in passing statutes in Hawaii and Nevada that allowed citizens to grow and smoke marijuana for "medical" purposes. States like Connecticut, New Mexico, and Wyoming, however, were not so easily fooled and rejected similar legislative efforts.

Not an Act of Compassion

Numerous other states are currently being targeted with various forms of legislation designed to medicalize, decriminalize, or legalize marijuana. Marijuana advocates count on legislators being ill-informed on this issue. However, the facts remain irrefutable.

Smoking marijuana cigarettes or inhaling marijuana smoke is not medicine!

Since the 1970s, the US Government has operated the Marijuana Research Center at the University of Mississippi. There they grow and process marijuana for research, monitoring marijuana research all over the world. The marijuana they provide is standardized, free of contamination, and consistent in potency. By January 2001, over 15,000 scientific, peer-reviewed research studies of marijuana had been published, and not one has shown marijuana to be a safe or effective medicine for any condition.

Smoking marijuana has been promoted as a "compassionate" move for the sick and dying . . . to assist people with cancer, AIDS, glaucoma, and Multiple Sclerosis. Yet, for each of these conditions, there already exist numerous safe and effective FDA [Food and Drug Administration] approved medications.

A California grower packages marijuana in labeled jars for medical use.

Legitimate medical organizations such as the American Medical Association, American Cancer society, National Multiple Sclerosis Association, American Academy of Ophthalmology, National Eye Institute, National Cancer Institute, National Institute for Neurological Disorders and Stroke, National Institute of Dental Research, and the National Institute on Allergy and Infectious Diseases state that marijuana has not been scientifically shown to be safe or effective as medicine. Legalizing marijuana through the political process bypasses the safeguards established by the Food and Drug Administration that have been established to protect the public from dangerous or ineffective drugs. Medicine must not be determined by political debate, but approved only after rigorous, peer-reviewed scientific research shows that it meets the legal criteria for therapeutic use.

Regardless of what a state may do toward legitimizing marijuana, the substance is still a Schedule I drug under the Controlled Substances Act, (21 USC 812), meaning, as a matter of law, (A) the drug has a high potential for abuse; (B) the drug has no current accepted medical use; and (C) the drug lacks accepted safety for use even under medical supervision. Possession, cultivation, and distribution remain illegal acts under federal law and international treaties to which the US is a signatory.

Dr. Robert DuPont, the former director of the National Institute on Drug Abuse, succinctly observed, ". . . Never in the history of modern medicine has burning leaves been considered medicine. Those of the medical marijuana movement are putting on white coats and expressing concerns about the sick. But people need to see this for what it is . . . a fraud and a hoax."

THREE

Marijuana Has Scientifically Proven Medical Benefits

Rob Kampia

Opponents of medical marijuana argue that marijuana has no therapeutic benefits and that its legalization could lead to an increase in recreational use of marijuana by young people. However, Rob Kampia argues in this selection that such opposition is based on falsehoods that can easily be refuted. Even the federally funded report by the Institute of Medicine conceded that smoking marijuana might provide relief for some patients, he notes. Unfortunately, he continues, the federal government resists scientific inquiry into the therapeutic benefits of medical marijuana and relies on falsehoods in making policy. Kampia concludes that the government should embrace a more objective, fact-based approach—one that relies on scientific evidence and research—to the issue of medical marijuana. Kampia is founder and executive director of the nonprofit organization Marijuana Policy Project, the largest marijuana policy reform organization in the United States.

I am executive director of the Marijuana Policy Project [MPP], the largest organization in the United States that is solely dedicated to ending marijuana prohibition. The Marijuana Policy Project has 15,000 dues-paying members and—as of today—nearly 70,000 e-

Rob Kampia, "Statement Before the House Committee on Government Reform, Subcommittee on Criminal Justice, Drug Policy, and Human Resources," CQ *Transcriptions*, April 1, 2004. Copyright © 2006 Congressional Quarterly Inc. All rights reserved. Reproduced by permission.

mail subscribers. (MPP's e-mail list is currently growing at the rate of 1,000 new names per day.) The Marijuana Policy Project works to minimize the harm associated with marijuana—both the consumption of marijuana and the laws that are intended to prohibit

Marijuana Can Relieve Chronic Health Problems

In a survey of fifty Canadian users of marijuana for medical purposes, the respondents reported that the drug helped to alleviate a variety of symptoms.

	Number of respondents who reported that their symptoms were relieved by the use of marijuana*
Problems sleeping	28
Loss of appetite	21
Nausea or pain (including menstrual cramps and headaches)	14
Depression	12
Anxiety/tension	11
Tics and muscular spasms	10
Seizures	4
Loss of energy	3
Difficulty breathing (asthma-related)	2
Craving for heroin	2
Anger	1
Eye irritation and double vision (in Graves Disease)	1

* Some respondents may have reported two or more symptoms.

Source: Adapted from the *Journal of Psychoactive Drugs*, October–December 2000, v. 32(4): 435–443. Alan C. Ogborne et al., Centre for Addiction and Mental Health, London, Ontario.

such use. MPP believes that the greatest harm associated with marijuana is imprisonment. The threat of imprisonment is especially dangerous and harmful when the individuals in question are seriously ill patients who use marijuana—with the approval of their physicians—to alleviate severe nausea, pain, muscle spasticity, and other debilitating medical conditions.

Welcoming a Science-Based Approach

But today's hearing is not designed to debate the moral implications of throwing cancer patients in prison when their doctors have agreed that marijuana is the best therapeutic option for them. Today we are here to talk about the science of medical marijuana. With respect to the title of this hearing, "Marijuana and Medicine: The Need for a Science-Based Approach," I would like to say upfront that the Marijuana Policy Project welcomes a "science-based approach" to this subject. In fact, we would celebrate such an approach because it would undoubtedly bring an end to the unnecessary and immoral federal attacks on doctors, patients, and caregivers who are acting legally under state law. Unfortunately, current federal policies are not based on science; rather, they are based on myths and lies. Worse yet, the federal government is currently blocking scientific inquiry into the therapeutic benefits of marijuana. This collusion in support of delusion is an outrage and must be stopped. State medical marijuana laws must be respected, and research into the therapeutic benefits of marijuana must be allowed to proceed expeditiously. The medical benefits of marijuana are widely recognized. Opponents of medical marijuana claim that marijuana has no medical benefits. The chairman of this subcommittee [Congressman Mark Souder, Indiana], gave a typical demonstration of this tactic in July 2003 during a debate on the House floor. During that debate he said that marijuana "does not help sick people. . . . There are no generally recognized health benefits to smoking marijuana."

The chairman, and those who agree with him, could not be more wrong. The appropriate starting point for demonstrating the inaccuracy of the chairman's claim is a 1999 report by the National

Academy of Sciences' Institute of Medicine entitled, "Marijuana and Medicine: Assessing the Science Base." This study was commissioned by the White House Office of National Drug Control Policy and directly addressed the question of smoked marijuana. It concluded in a section entitled, "Use of Smoked Marijuana": "It will likely be many years before a safe and effective cannabinoid delivery system, such as an inhaler, is available for patients. In the meantime, there are patients with debilitating symptoms for whom smoked marijuana might provide relief." The principal investigator of this study added at the news conference at which

A member of a California medical marijuana co-operative lights up his daily dose.

the report was released, "[W]e concluded that there are some limited circumstances in which we recommend smoking marijuana for medical uses." It is unfortunate that the authors of this study are not here to testify today. The recognition of marijuana's medical benefits goes well beyond the Institute of Medicine. For those familiar with the scheduling of controlled substances, marijuana is a Schedule I drug, which is defined as having "no currently accepted medical use," while Schedule II drugs are defined as having a "currently accepted medical use." Therefore, anyone who suggests that marijuana should not be a Schedule I drug believes that it has generally recognized health benefits.

What the Medical Experts Say

With this in mind, let's review what some medical professionals say about marijuana. An editorial in the *New England Journal of Medicine*—while calling the federal war on medical marijuana patients "misguided, heavy-handed, and inhumane"—suggested that the government "should change marijuana's status from that of a Schedule I drug to a Schedule II drug and regulate it accordingly." In June 2003, the 2.6 million-member American Nurses Association passed a resolution supporting the rescheduling of marijuana out of Schedule I. The American Public Health Association [APHA], the oldest and largest organization of health professionals in the world, "overwhelmingly" adopted a resolution concluding, "Marijuana was wrongfully placed in Schedule I." In this resolution, the APHA noted that marijuana has been reported to be effective in (1) reducing the intraocular pressure caused by glaucoma, (2) reducing the nausea and vomiting associated with chemotherapy, (3) stimulating the appetite of patients living with AIDS and suffering from wasting syndrome, (4) controlling the spasticity that is associated with spinal cord injuries and multiple sclerosis, (5) decreasing the suffering from chronic pain, and (6) controlling seizures associated with seizure disorders. Even non-political government officials have supported the rescheduling of marijuana. In 1988, the DEA's [Drug Enforcement Administration] chief administrative law judge, Francis L. Young,

This cannabis plant is being cultivated at a federal government–sponsored research farm at the University of Mississippi.

ruled: "Marijuana, in its natural form, is one of the safest therapeutically active substances known . . . [T]he provisions of the [Controlled Substances] Act permit and require the transfer of marijuana from Schedule I to Schedule II. It would be unreasonable, arbitrary and capricious for DEA to continue to stand between those sufferers and the benefits of this substance." . . .

The Federal Government Is Blocking Research

It is disturbing that some members of Congress are unwilling to acknowledge the overwhelming evidence that marijuana has recognized medical uses. But it is even more offensive that these members of Congress sit idly as the executive branch of the federal government blocks research into the therapeutic benefits of marijuana. If this subcommittee is truly interested in a science-based approach to marijuana's therapeutic uses, it should use its authority and influence to help remove the barriers to this research.

Here are some examples of how the federal government has impeded research on the therapeutic benefits of marijuana: In December 1999, the U.S. Department of Health and Human Services (HHS) established guidelines that researchers must follow if they wish to study the therapeutic benefits of marijuana. These guidelines place a much greater burden on medical marijuana researchers than on drug companies that develop and study newly synthesized pharmaceuticals. For example, HHS's guidelines require marijuana

A laboratory technician displays a cannabis bud (left) used to produce the pharmaceutical drug Marinol (right) for use instead of smoking pot.

research protocols to undergo a review by an ad hoc, marijuana-specific panel within HHS, which is in addition to FDA approval of the protocols. This is an unnecessary and cumbersome hurdle that pharmaceutical companies do not face. Medical marijuana researchers should not receive special treatment, but they should receive equal and fair treatment. In November 1999, more than 30 U.S. representatives sent a letter to HHS Secretary Donna Shalala, urging her to promulgate guidelines that would simply treat marijuana research like research on any other drug.

Second, the National Institute on Drug Abuse [NIDA] currently has a monopoly on the cultivation of marijuana for research in the United States. Unfortunately, NIDA's marijuana is only available for research, not for prescriptive use. Therefore, how could a pharmaceutical company be expected to invest millions of dollars in researching a product that it could not eventually sell on the market? Can you imagine any private firm conducting research under these conditions? Moreover, there have been many complaints about the quality of NIDA's marijuana. Five U.S. representatives sent a letter to the DEA in support of an alternative source of research-grade marijuana, expressing concerns such as those described in this paragraph. Finally, the Drug Enforcement Administration has played its own important role in blocking medical marijuana research. For nearly three years, the DEA has delayed action on an application from the University of Massachusetts for a license to cultivate marijuana for federally approved research. In fact, the comment period on this application closed more than six months ago [in mid-2003]. Yet the DEA still has not approved or rejected this application. The proposed production facility is needed because—as described above—NIDA's monopoly is preventing effective research from moving forward. . . .

Opposition Based on Falsehoods

As noted, there is almost no way that a science-based approach can lead to the conclusion that marijuana—even smoked marijuana—is not medicine. The opposition to medical marijuana isn't based on science, but rather lies and myths that are refutable by indisputable facts. The lead mythmakers with respect to medical marijuana are the officials at ONDCP [Office of National Drug Control Policy]. Here are a couple of good examples, both taken from a column by ONDCP Deputy Director Andrea Barthwell, published in the *Chicago Tribune* on February 17, 2004. The first is related to Marinol, the prescription drug that contains a synthetic version of one of the active ingredients in marijuana—THC. Barthwell wrote that "marijuana advocates refuse to acknowledge Marinol as a viable option. Interestingly enough, the only property that Marinol lacks is the ability to create a 'high.'" Barthwell's assertions about Marinol are false. First, Marinol most certainly produces a high. This is stated clearly in the *Physician's Desk Reference* [PDR]. In the list of adverse reactions on page 3326, the very first entry is "a cannabinoid dose-related 'high.'" This high is enough of a concern that the *PDR* warns, "Patients receiving treatment with Marinol should be specifically warned not to drive, operate machinery or engage in any hazardous activity until it is established that they are able to tolerate the drug and perform such tasks safely." And, to contradict another of Barthwell's claims, natural marijuana has at least two properties that Marinol lacks: Rapid onset of action, and superior control over dosage. As noted in the article "Therapeutic Potential of Cannabis," in the May 2003 issue of *The Lancet Neurology*, "Oral administration is probably the least satisfactory route for cannabis." The journal noted that the oral route "makes dose titration more difficult and therefore increases the potential for adverse psychoactive effects." Barthwell got the science exactly backwards.

Marijuana and Teens

The second myth Barthwell propounded in her op-ed is the claim that allowing seriously ill patients to use medical marijuana somehow increases teenage marijuana use. In fact, research has shown otherwise. In California, marijuana use by teens was rising until the 1996 passage of Proposition 215, the medical marijuana law.

Former U.S. surgeon general Jocelyn Elders has refuted common myths about why marijuana should not be used for medicine.

After that law took effect, teen marijuana use in California dropped dramatically over the next six years—as much as 40% in some age groups. . . . A special analysis commissioned by the California state government found absolutely no evidence that Prop. 215 had increased teen marijuana use. Both of Barthwell's myths were refuted in a [March 2004] op-ed in the *Providence [RI] Journal* by former U.S. Surgeon General Joycelyn Elders. She also addressed some other common myths, such as "Marijuana is too dangerous to be medicine. It's bad for the immune system, endangering AIDS and cancer patients," and "Smoke is not medicine. No real medicine is smoked." With respect to the latter myth, Dr. Elders offered the following: "The truth: Marijuana does not need to be smoked. Some patients prefer to eat it, while those who need the fast action and dose control provided by inhalation can avoid the hazards of smoke through simple devices called vaporizers. For many who need only a small amount—like cancer patients simply trying to get through a few months of chemotherapy—the risks of smoking are minor." Regarding the claim that marijuana is too dangerous to be a medicine, it is interesting to note that there has never been a death attributed to an overdose of marijuana. Clearly, most prescription drugs are far more dangerous than marijuana. Even over-the-counter drugs like aspirin and Tylenol cause numerous overdose deaths each year.

A Federal Witch Hunt

Since we are accustomed to responding to misconceptions about medical marijuana, the Marijuana Policy Project has prepared factual responses to 33 common challenges to marijuana's therapeutic uses. These responses can be found in the document, "Effective Arguments for Medical Marijuana Advocates." Anyone opposed to the medical use of marijuana should read this document before arguing publicly against its use in the future. This hearing is a witch hunt, not a quest for knowledge. The goal of this subcommittee, under its current leadership, is not to adopt a true scientific approach to the subject of marijuana. If that were the case, the authors of the Institute of Medicine report and physicians and patients from the eight medical marijuana states would have been invited. Or a representative from the American Nurses Association. Or a representative from the American Public Health Association. No, the clear goal of the current chairman is to expend federal funds in a fruitless quest to find evidence that supports his own baseless belief. For example, the panel I'm speaking on is composed of representatives from two state boards that are currently investigating possible wrongdoing under state medical marijuana laws, even though no wrongdoing has been established. The chairman also invited two physicians whose activities have come into question, while ignoring the thousands of physicians who have recommended marijuana to their patients under state law without controversy. Finally, the chairman invited Mr. [Robert] DuPont, [president, Institute for Behavior and Health], whose value as a witness seems to be that he is one of the leading medical marijuana mythmakers.

But this is not the first time Chairman Souder has expended government funds to "expose" medical marijuana. In June 2001, Chairman Souder requested, on behalf of the subcommittee, that the General Accounting Office [GAO] investigate state medical marijuana programs. At taxpayer expense, the GAO traveled to Alaska, California, Hawaii, and Oregon to carry out this request. When this lengthy report was completed in November 2002, it contained few, if any, controversial findings. The researchers commented generally on the small number of patients who are registered, and the paucity of doctors who are recommending marijuana as a treatment option. Even the law-enforcement officials interviewed for the report seemed to be unfazed by state medical marijuana laws. Most of the 37 selected law enforcement organizations interviewed in the report "indicated that medical marijuana laws had had little impact on their law enforcement activities for a variety of reasons." Nearly two-thirds of these law enforcement officials did not believe that "the introduction of medical marijuana laws have, or could make it, more difficult to pursue or prosecute some marijuana cases." And nearly three-quarters of these officials denied that "there has been a general softening in public attitude toward marijuana or public perception that marijuana is no longer illegal."

In sum, the Marijuana Policy Project strongly supports a science-based approach to medical marijuana. We hope that chairman Souder eventually abandons his reliance on myths and lies, stops the federal witch hunt for medical marijuana patients and doctors, and embraces an approach that is based on science.

FOUR

The Harms of Marijuana May Outweigh the Medical Benefits

Physicians for a Smoke-Free Canada

Physicians for a Smoke-Free Canada (PSC) is an organization of Canadian physicians that seeks the reduction of tobacco-caused illnesses through reduced smoking and decreased exposure to secondhand smoke. In the following article PSC criticizes the Canadian government's plan to make medical marijuana available to patients. First, not enough is known about the chemical components of marijuana to justify allowing research subjects to inhale marijuana smoke, PSC insists, especially when there is evidence that marijuana smoke damages the lungs in much the same way as tobacco smoke does. Second, under the plan, physicians would be allowed to prescribe marijuana to qualifying patients. However, most physicians lack the knowledge or experience to match doses with symptoms. These issues should be resolved before the government adopts any new medical marijuana policies, PSC argues.

Health Canada, [the Canadian government's health department] is making marijuana available to an increasing number of ailing Canadians through a new regulatory agenda. Unfortunately, both of the main components of the new agen-

"Health Canada's Policies on Marijuana Put Patients at Risk," *Physicians for a Smoke-Free Canada*, January 2002, reproduced by permission.

da—the research plan and the exemption plan—fail to either draw or adhere to appropriate boundaries.

This lack of boundaries is due in part to a lack of thorough knowledge about the drug—while claims and testimonials about the benefits of marijuana abound, crucial information about its active chemical components and their specific benefits remain unknown. At this point in time, we know more about the harm caused by marijuana smoke than we do about the benefits.

Risks from Inhaling Smoke

Numerous studies have found that marijuana smoke produces pulmonary damage similar to that produced by tobacco smoke, only more severe. Major health agencies, including Health Canada, the American National Institutes of Health, and the Institutes of Medicine, have all recognized the severity of these risks in their informational reviews.

Handelsman. © 1993 by Tribune Media Services, Inc. Reproduced by permission.

Despite their written recognition of the health risks associated with smoking marijuana, however, Health Canada is funding clinical trials of smoked marijuana under its medical marijuana research plan. In fact, the plan's call for proposals explicitly states that studies of smoked marijuana will be given funding priority over studies of non-smoked cannabinoids.

Because of the health risks entailed in such research, Health Canada does stipulate that studies and trials should be restricted

A Canadian AIDS patient displays his first shipment of medical marijuana (and the bill for it) that he received through the national health service, Health Canada.

to, "short-term, self-limiting symptomatic conditions" (that is, conditions which should clear up relatively quickly by themselves, such as common colds). Nonetheless, currently funded studies include trials for conditions which are neither short-term nor self-limiting. At McGill University, for example, researchers are studying the effects of smoked marijuana on patients with chronic neuropathic pain.

This is especially worrisome since the terms in which Health Canada's research plan is laid out do not guarantee that participants will be warned adequately about the risks they are assuming by smoking the drug.

Risks from Inadequate Research

The lack of appropriate boundaries in the medical marijuana research plan is mirrored in the medical marijuana exemption plan. Under this plan, any patient for whom conventional treatments have failed or been deemed inappropriate can apply for an exemption to the Controlled Drug and Substances Act's prohibition on marijuana. In order for an application to be successful, the applicant's treating physician must prescribe a daily dosage and state that in the applicant's case the benefits of treatment with marijuana outweigh the risks.

This presents a number of problems for physicians. First, since marijuana has not been thoroughly tested as a medicine, most physicians are familiar neither with its potential benefits (if any), nor with the dosage required to achieve those benefits. Second, when a patient is requesting smoked marijuana, the risks associated with smoking, coupled with the lack of clinical knowledge about specific benefits, make any accurate approximation of the risk-to-benefit ratio of treatment impossible.

Until the contradictions and ambiguities written into Health Canada's new policies on marijuana are addressed, patients, trial participants, and physicians will all be at risk.

FIVE

Legalizing Medical Marijuana Would Negatively Impact Society

Mark R. Trouville

> Legalizing medical marijuana would interfere with and undermine law enforcement efforts to combat drug trafficking and would send a dangerous message that marijuana is a harmless substance, Mark R. Trouville writes in this selection taken from his testimony before the Vermont State House Committee on Health and Welfare. Trouville insists that statistics and studies clearly demonstrate that marijuana is not harmless. Though further research into the medicinal benefits of isolated components of marijuana is warranted, he concedes, there is currently no established scientific or medical consensus that marijuana has therapeutic value. Trouville currently serves as the special agent in charge of the Miami field division of the Drug Enforcement Administration, where he oversees all operations throughout the state of Florida as well as the Bahamas.

The overwhelming weight of evidence and experience conclusively show that marijuana and its consequences are dangerous to both users and non-users. The Drug Enforcement Administration (DEA) therefore vigilantly enforces federal laws prohibiting manufacturing and distribution of marijuana. We believe that the proposal before you today [S. 76, "The Medical

Mark R. Trouville, "Statement Before the Vermont House Committee on Health and Welfare," April 14, 2004. Reproduced by permission.

Use of Marijuana"], would have a significant negative impact on federal enforcement. It is not only inconsistent with federal law, it obstructs federal law. We have seen from experience in other states that state laws permitting use of marijuana encourage violations of federal law and pose significant practical obstacles to law enforcement. Moreover, we do not believe that the proposal will accomplish its stated goals because, as the Institute of Medicine (IOM) put it, "[t]here is little future in smoked marijuana as a medically approved medication." On balance, the potentially significant negative impact on public health and safety as well as law enforcement should weigh heavily against this legislation. We believe the citizens of Vermont will be best served by keeping state law consistent with the view Congress has settled upon based on the weight of scientific and medical evidence. [S. 76 passed the state Senate on a 22-7 vote but stalled in committee in the House].

Legalizing Medical Marijuana Will Undermine Law Enforcement

While states are free to define criminal acts and impose corresponding penalties in the manner they see fit, it does not follow

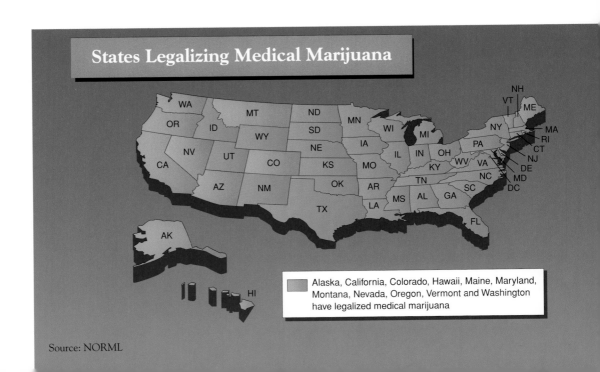

States Legalizing Medical Marijuana

Alaska, California, Colorado, Hawaii, Maine, Maryland, Montana, Nevada, Oregon, Vermont and Washington have legalized medical marijuana

Source: NORML

that the absence of state penalties "legalizes" conduct that remains unlawful under federal law. More than seven years of experience have demonstrated that when a state legalizes marijuana under its law, residents are effectively encouraged to violate federal drug laws. This result undermines the protection to the public health and safety inherent in the federal drug approval process, creates public confusion, interferes with law enforcement efforts to combat drug trafficking, and runs afoul of the Supremacy Clause of the United States Constitution.

This is not rhetoric—let me illustrate these very real problems from the DEA's experience in other states. For example, two investigations involving "medical" marijuana clubs demonstrate that purported "medical" use only hides everyday drug dealing. The clubs' owners cultivated and distributed significant amounts of "medical" marijuana in the area, not only to "patients," but to anyone who wanted to buy it. In one of the investigations, a witness claims to have seen more than 4,000 plants being cultivated inside one of the clubs. In the second case, approximately 979 plants and several pounds of processed marijuana were seized during the execution of a Federal search warrant. One of the owners admitted that he rented the property and grew the marijuana for his 120 "patients." In addition to the contraband that was seized, documents indicating that the grower had made $140,000 in profits from his drug dealing were also seized.

Along these lines, I would like to point out that the bill before you today is conspicuously silent with regard to the fact that the cultivation, distribution, and possession of marijuana, even in compliance with the bill, would violate federal law and subject the individuals engaged in such conduct to criminal and civil prosecution. That omission points to a glaring practical issue in the legislation—there is simply no way for it to be given effect without encouraging and facilitating trafficking in a federally controlled substance.

When the General Assembly considers this proposal, we hope it will consider how these types of laws undermine the efforts of law enforcement officials at every level nationwide. In the states that have passed these types of laws since 1996, longtime drug dealers have reinvented themselves as "caregivers" so that they can claim immunity from prosecution. This proposal and similar laws enacted in other states are written in a manner that makes it easy for any drug dealer to concoct a "medical" marijuana defense. The impact on law enforcement should be obvious. As a Maryland lawyer recently was publicly quoted as saying, there "are a whole bunch of people who like marijuana who can now try to use this defense."

Marijuana Use Is Dangerous to the User and Others

The DEA vigilantly enforces federal laws against marijuana trafficking for a simple reason that remains as compelling, if not more compelling, today than in the past: marijuana use is dangerous to both the user and the non-user, particularly children. This is true irrespective of whether or not its use is for purported "medical" purposes. While the list of these concerns is lengthy, I would like to highlight the most telling examples.

Marijuana is the most widely used illicit drug in America and a widespread social and human service concern. More young people are currently in treatment for marijuana dependency than for alcohol and all other illegal drugs combined, and mentions of marijuana use in emergency room visits have risen 176 percent since 1994, surpassing those of heroin. Any liberalization of marijuana policy will send a false and misleading message that marijuana is harmless if not affirmatively good for you, exacerbating the already significant problem of marijuana abuse. Use of marijuana by young people is a frequent precursor to the use of more dangerous drugs, and signals a significantly enhanced likelihood of drug problems in adult life. For example, a study done by the Substance Abuse and Mental Health Services Administration (SAMHSA) in 2002 found that 62 percent of the adults who first tried marijuana before they were 15 years old were likely to go on to cocaine—but the same was true of only one-half of one percent of adults who had never tried marijuana.

Smoked marijuana is also dangerous to those who use it, belying any beneficent rationale in permitting its use. Marijuana smoke contains 50 percent to 70 percent more carcinogenic hydrocarbons than tobacco smoke. Marijuana may promote cancer of the respiratory tract and provide heightened risk of lung infection and many other diseases. The British Medical Association (BMA) is so concerned about the negative health impact of liberalization initiatives such as the one before you today that it recently voiced "extreme concern" that altering the criminal penalties for mari-

Drug Enforcement Administration agents remove marijuana from a San Francisco dispensary where it was slated to be distributed to medical patients.

juana use would create a misleading impression that marijuana is safe to use that the BMA emphasized that "the public must be made aware of the harmful effects we know result from smoking the drug."

As DEA Administrator [Karen] Tandy repeatedly emphasizes, the significance of maintaining cohesive and coordinated laws against marijuana use is the harm it causes to the non-user, which is in no way reduced when use of the drug is for claimed "medical" purposes. One compelling example is drugged driving. Marijuana affects alertness, concentration, perception, coordination, and reaction time—skills that are necessary for safe driving. A roadside study of reckless drivers in Tennessee found that 33 percent of those tested who were not under the influence of alcohol tested positive for marijuana. Although this bill specifically exempts drugged driving from its protection, there can be little serious doubt that any increase in use will proportionally increase drugged driving. Use of marijuana and other illicit drugs also comes at significant expense to society in terms of lost employee productivity, public health care costs, and accidents. Finally, research shows a link between frequent marijuana use and increased violent behavior, and young people who use marijuana weekly are nearly four times more likely than non-users to engage in violence.

Smoked Marijuana Is Not Medicine

Supporters of liberalization of marijuana laws attempt to balance these demonstrable and widespread social harms and health risks against purported benefits for a few users for claimed "medical" purposes. The evidence is clear, however, that smoked marijuana not only has "little future" as medicine, as the IOM put it, but that there is not established scientific and medical proof that marijuana has therapeutic value.

It is clear to DEA that there is no consensus on the medical evidence that smoking marijuana helps patients. The American Medical Association has rejected pleas to endorse smoked marijuana as medicine, and instead has urged that marijuana remain a "Schedule I" drug (which by definition has no accepted medical use) pending further research. The National Multiple Sclerosis Society has concluded that existing studies "have not provided convincing evidence that marijuana benefits people with MS," further emphasizing that "marijuana is not recommended as a treatment" and that "long-term use of marijuana may be associated with significant side effects."

Just as importantly, marijuana has not been approved for use as a "medicine" under the rigorous federal drug approval process conducted by the Food and Drug Administration as required by law. That process prohibits any drug from being sold as a medicine unless it has been proven in sound clinical studies to be both safe and effective for its intended use. To date, no sound scientific study has shown that smoking marijuana is both safe and effective for any disease or condition. Our medical system relies on proven scientific research, not polling results or supposition.

The federal government continues, however, to support research into the medical efficacy of certain isolated properties and ingredients of marijuana. One such example is Marinol, which is a safe, pill form of synthetic THC that has been effective in promoting health without delivering all the harmful substances that are found in smoked marijuana. The DEA has approved and will continue to approve research into whether there may be other appropriate uses for THC or other specific ingredients of marijuana. But even if smoking marijuana makes people "feel better," that is not enough to call it a "medicine" any more than one would suggest using heroin to treat a sick person. Medicine must be defined by scientists and physicians and not lobbyists, and compassion dictates that harmful drugs should not be touted as medicine to an unsuspecting public.

SIX

Legalizing Medical Marijuana May Not Negatively Impact Society

Shereen Khatapoush and Denise Hallfors

Recent state initiatives legalizing medical marijuana have renewed the national debate about whether legalization could mislead young people into thinking marijuana is safe, resulting in increased recreational use among teenagers. Because of this concern, a study was designed to examine attitudes and drug use in California and ten other states. The study was based on telephone surveys that were conducted in 1995, 1997, and 1999 (before and after California passed Proposition 215 in 1996). In the following excerpt authors Shereen Khatapoush and Denise Hallfors describe the study and conclude that concerns about sending the wrong message to young people may be overstated. Though participants in the survey did not believe marijuana was harmful, this belief did not manifest itself in increased drug use. In addition, attitudes about and use of marijuana did not result in the so-called gateway to harder drugs. Despite these results, the authors conclude it is too early to tell whether the legalization of medical marijuana will influence public attitudes in the long run. For this reason, more research is needed, especially if other states decide to legalize marijuana for medical purposes. Khatapoush is an associate research scientist at Prevention Research Center in

Shereen Khatapoush and Denise Hallfors, "Sending the Wrong Message: Did Medical Marijuana Legalization in California Change Attitudes About and Use of Marijuana?" *Journal of Drug Issues*, vol. 34, Fall 2004. Republished with permission of *Journal of Drug Issues*, conveyed through Copyright Clearance Center Inc.

Berkeley, California. She has worked in substance abuse prevention for more than ten years and is interested in youth, prevention, and policy. Hallfors is a senior research scientist at the Pacific Institute for Research and Evaluation in Chapel Hill, North Carolina. She has a background in nursing, with doctoral training from the Heller School at Brandeis University. She has done extensive research on adolescent substance abuse prevention.

Marijuana policy has been a contentious issue in the United States. Over time, federal marijuana policy has become increasingly restrictive and punitive, while state policy has been more fluid and lax. Recently, citizen-sponsored state referenda to legalize marijuana for medicinal purposes have challenged federal policy, sparking a national debate. Critics have argued that medicinal use "sends the wrong message" to youth. The purpose of this [viewpoint] is to test this argument by examining marijuana attitudes and behaviors before and after a seminal California law was passed.

From "Zero Tolerance" to "Compassionate Use"

Current federal drug policy can be characterized as a "zero tolerance" approach, with primary emphasis on supply reduction, enforcement strategies, and legal sanctions. Historically, federal marijuana policy began with the Marijuana Tax Act of 1937 and became more restrictive over time with the passage of the Boggs Act and the Narcotic Control Act during the 1950's. The Boggs Act established uniform penalties and mandatory minimum sentencing and the Narcotic Control Act escalated the penalties and fines for the possession and sale of narcotics and made other provisions and guidelines for the enforcement of narcotic laws (including marijuana). Despite the harsher penalties that were enacted in the mid-1950s, recreational marijuana use not only continued, but increased dramatically during the 1960s. In 1970, the Controlled Substances Act classified marijuana as a Schedule I drug (along with heroin and LSD), meaning that it had a high

Luckovich © by *Atlanta Constitution*. Reproduced by permission of Mike Luckovich and Creators Syndicate, Inc.

potential for abuse, no accepted medical utility, lack of accepted safety for use even under medical supervision, and was subject to the most stringent regulatory controls. Despite these increasingly elevated sanctions over time, recreational use and the corresponding costs associated with marijuana enforcement increased, and efforts to relax federal policies since the 1970s, such as rescheduling marijuana, have failed.

Although states are subject to federal law, most have experimented with their own policy approaches. During the late 1960s and 1970s, almost all states reduced the penalties for marijuana use. By the end of 1971, only three states maintained mandatory minimum felony penalties for possession. Oregon was the first state to decriminalize marijuana in 1973; by 1978, twelve additional states, with collectively more than a third of the total U.S. population, had done so. Californians passed the Moscone Act in 1976, which decriminalized possession of marijuana and removed prison sentences. For the next 20 years, until the medical marijuana initiative was passed in 1996, California's marijuana laws did not change substantially.

In November 1996, California voters passed Proposition 215, the Compassionate Use Act, which allows patients to cultivate and use marijuana for medicinal purposes with the written or oral recommendation of a doctor. A number of other states have since passed medical marijuana initiatives. These state initiatives clearly conflict with federal policy and much of the concern and opposition has been centered around the notion that allowing medicinal use would "send the wrong message" to youth—that is, change attitudes and perceptions about marijuana and result in

This medical marijuana store in San Francisco offers a variety of cannabis products for use only by state-approved medical patients.

greater recreational use of marijuana and other illicit drugs. Comments made by General Barry McCaffrey, former director of the White House Office of National Drug Control Policy, typify this concern:

> These measures threaten to undermine our efforts to protect our children from dangerous psychoactive drugs. They make drug abuse more likely. Marijuana is a "gateway" drug. Children who have used marijuana are more than 85 times likelier to use cocaine than children who have never used marijuana. They send the wrong message to our children. Coming at a time when marijuana use has doubled among our youth, these initiatives threaten to undermine our efforts to prevent drug use by our children. We cannot afford to further erode youth attitudes towards drugs by allowing marijuana to be falsely depicted as a safe drug and as effective medicine. Labeling marijuana as "medicine" sends the wrong message to children that it is a safe substance. What is at risk is the well-being of our nation's youth.

The Institute of Medicine Study

In response to these and other concerns about the medical use of marijuana, the federal government commissioned a study by the Institute of Medicine (IOM). In its final report, the commission noted:

> Almost everyone who spoke or wrote to the IOM study team about the potential harms posed by the medical use of marijuana felt that it would send the wrong message to children and teenagers. They stated that information about the harms caused by marijuana is undermined by claims that marijuana might have medical value. Yet many of our powerful medicines are also dangerous medicines . . . The question here is not whether marijuana can be both harmful and helpful, but whether the perception of its benefits will increase its abuse. For now any answer to the question remains conjecture.

The IOM report went on to suggest, however, that "reasonable inferences" could be drawn from the medical use and abuse of opiates, the effects of marijuana decriminalization and the short-term consequences of the medical marijuana campaign in California. . . . After highlighting the findings in these areas, they concluded, "no convincing data support . . . the broad social concern that sanctioning the medical use of marijuana might lead to an increase in its use among the general population." The purpose of this study is to empirically assess whether enacting more liberal state policies: (1) changes attitudes, decreasing beliefs that marijuana is harmful, increasing perceived availability and increasing approval for use; (2) changes behavior, increasing marijuana use, and, based on gateway theory, (3) changes other "hard" drug use behavior.

The theoretical and empirical literature suggests that, as with most complex human behavior and social problems, substance abuse is best explained in terms of the interaction of numerous personal and environmental factors. Research indicates that personal attitudes are correlated and interact with other variables to help predict behavior. There also appears to be a general sequence in drug use, and progression to a particular drug is influenced not only by age of initiation and previous "softer" drug use, but also by a number of other personal and environmental factors. Taking this literature into consideration, we might not expect marijuana policy change to have a significant effect on youth. It is important, however, given the social concern and lack of studies in this area, to examine the impact of policy change and to assess whether it produced negative outcomes. . . .

Results and Implications

We found that while perceptions of harm from marijuana use have decreased over time in California and in other states, marijuana and other drug use has remained stable. Though support for medical use and general legalization of marijuana has increased over time in other states, personal approval for recreational use has decreased and use has not changed.

Activists for California's Proposition 215, allowing medical use of marijuana, staff an information table on the initiative before voters approved it in 1996.

A major concern was that legalizing medical marijuana would "send the wrong message to youth" and lead to greater drug use. Since use did not increase, these arguments are not supported. Respondents in this study increasingly believed that marijuana was not terribly harmful. However, this was not coupled with increased use, and approval for personal recreational use decreased, even while support for medical use increased. One might argue that policy changes did in fact "send the wrong message," since perceived harm decreased, and youth and young adults in other states' policy attitudes became more liberal. However, there is a conceptual, and this research suggests an empirical, distinction between attitudes that may relate to recreational use versus those that relate to medical use/policy. Even while perceived harm decreased and support for medical legalization increased, approval for use decreased and actual use did not change. Therefore, it may be that changes in perceived harm have more to do with policy attitudes, and changes in approval have more to do with recreational use, since use remained stable across the country. Moreover, since six states passed medical marijuana initiatives between 1997 and 2000, we would expect, and indeed found, in all but California, attitudes about policy became more liberal over time. That is, on the whole, attitudes were not changing over time in California but were changing in other states. Therefore, one implication of our results may be that policy changes reflect attitude changes, rather than policy causing attitude changes.

Another implication is that other states may be converging with California. Attitudes are typically more liberal (and use higher) in the West, and in California in particular, compared to the rest of the country. The majority of Americans still oppose the idea of legalized marijuana. Americans see drugs as a serious problem nationally, but not in their local area. Liberal attitudes may have led to policy changes in California; although attitudes have since been stable in California, they have been changing in other states, while policy was also changing. Thus, California can be viewed as a bellwether state. However, in order to fully test the direction and association of attitudes and policy change, longitudinal data with representative state samples are needed, with data collection both before and after policy change.

Comparing Results

The results of this study indicate that marijuana and other illicit drug use remained stable in the latter part of the 1990s; these results are validated by other recent findings. The most recent Monitoring the Future (MTF) data indicate that adolescent use has remained stable or decreased in the last few years. Similarly, National Household Survey on Drug Abuse (NHSDA) data indicate little change in marijuana use among 12 to 26 year olds between 1997 and 1999. Moreover, as in the present study, the NHSDA data indicate a decline in perceived risk of harm from marijuana use. Finally, the Harvard College Alcohol Study found that past-month marijuana use among college students increased from 1993 to 1999 but that nearly all of the change had occurred by 1997. Thus, the results of this study are consistent with other recent research on youth and young adult marijuana use.

How do these findings compare to other studies about the relationship between marijuana attitudes and use? Previous analyses of MTF data suggested that changes in marijuana use are closely correlated with perceived harm and approval. However, in the present study, although harm and approval were significantly associated with use, they were moving in different directions. It is possible that although Proposition 215 and the ongoing debate did not change attitudes and thus affect use, the policy change and debate may have altered the relationship between attitudes and use. Examination of correlations between attitudes and use over time suggest that the relationship between attitudes and use has in fact changed. Correlations between use, availability, harm, and approval became weaker over time. This suggests that attitudes about availability, harm, and approval may be becoming somewhat less salient to actual use of marijuana. One perplexing finding here was that Californians indicated less approval for occasional marijuana use, but higher use rates. Likewise, respondents in other states indicated higher approval for use, but less actual use of marijuana. It may be that this finding is an artifact of our data, or it may be another indication that the relationship between attitudes and use is complex and changing. The results further suggest that people distinguish between recreational and medical use: they can believe marijuana is not greatly harmful and approve of legalization for medical use but still disapprove of personal use. Further research is clearly needed to explore and explain the relationship between attitudes and use, the impact of policy changes on this relationship, and the impact of policy changes on use.

Medical Marijuana Does Not Send the Wrong Message

In light of gateway theory and the historically greater risk of progression to other illicit drug use among marijuana users, how do we understand the apparently short-lived but marked increase in marijuana but not other drug use in the 1990s? Should we be concerned that higher rates of initiation and use of marijuana in the mid 1990s may yet lead to greater other illicit drug use? Two recent and related studies by Golub and Johnson help clarify these issues. In the first of these studies, they examine probabilities of drug use progression and their covariates and conclude, "The recent increase in youthful marijuana use has been offset by lower rates of progression to hard drug use among youths born in the 1970s. Dire predictions of future hard drug abuse by youths who came of age in the 1990s may be greatly overstated." In a study for the National Institute of Justice, which included both the criminal and general populations, they conclude:

> A standing argument for controlling marijuana use, based on the gateway theory, is that it can lead to the use of more dangerous drugs. As determined in this study, however, the drug of choice for persons born in the 1970's and coming of

A San Francisco cannabis club member lights a joint after the club was reopened following legal battles over the medicinal use of marijuana.

age in the 1990's has been marijuana. These youths have been much less prone to progress to other drugs than their predecessors. This suggests that the gateway theory may be less relevant to their experience.

Furthermore, although the number of new marijuana initiates aged 12–17 was increasing in the early 1990's, this trend peaked in 1995 and the number of new marijuana initiates declined each year thereafter.

The available data suggest that the changes in marijuana policy did not "send the wrong message" and lead to greater drug use. Why might this be so? Consider the content of the message—imbedded in the debates, the controversy—that marijuana is an illegal substance. The very fact that there was a debate highlighted the tension between possible medical benefit while reminding the public that marijuana is illegal, to say nothing of the message sent by actions of federal agencies, such as raids on distribution centers, threatening doctors with revocation of their DEA prescription authority, criminal prosecution, and exclusion from participation in Medicare and Medicaid programs, and prosecution of anyone involved with medical marijuana under federal law.

Moreover, the policy change and associated debate may have sent some "message" but not one we would expect to dramatically change marijuana-related attitudes and use because the relationship between attitudes and behaviors is complex, as is drug use behavior. Various attitudes have a differing relationship to use, and attitudes are not the only influences on drug use. Moreover, research suggests that attitudes are helpful in predicting behavior to the extent that they are aggregated, well matched to the behavior in question, and when they are based on personal experience and substantial information. Policy-related attitudes about medical legalization likely have not had an impact on drug use behavior because these variables, together or separately, are not well matched or explicitly linked to youth recreational marijuana use, and therefore did not alter recreational use norms and behavior. Finally, what we know about the etiology [the study of the causes of diseases] of drug use suggests that drug use is complex and is influenced by numerous factors, some more proximal and personal, and others more distal, contextual, or environmental. Medical marijuana policy is a relatively distal factor, compared to other variables that are important in predicting marijuana use, such as individual risk factors and social influence. Thus, despite the considerable media attention and public discussion and debate about legalizing medical marijuana, the policy change and associated issues may have been sufficiently irrelevant and/or ambivalent to produce changes in youth and young adult marijuana-related attitudes and use. . . .

Full Effects of Policy Change Yet to Be Determined

This research suggests that medical marijuana policy has had little impact on youth and young adult marijuana-related attitudes and use in selected communities across the country. The ultimate outcome measure in this study was marijuana use, and it remained stable from 1995 to 1999.

[According to a Gallup poll conducted in 2000], medical marijuana continues to be part of public dialogue and debate nationally and internationally. As of August 2003, nine states (with more than 20% of the U.S. population) allow medical marijuana use, and Canada recently legalized medical use. Nearly three out of four Americans (73%) favor legalization for medical purposes, less than one third (31%) support general legalization of marijuana and the country is nearly evenly split on whether marijuana possession should be treated as a criminal offense. Regardless of public opinion, however, marijuana is a controlled substance, and recreational use, although decriminalized in some states, is still illegal.

Clearly, more research is needed on the impact of medical marijuana policy and how this may relate to nonmedical marijuana-related attitudes and use. In a review of marijuana policy issues in the U.S. and Australia, Single and colleagues (2000) conclude:

Regardless of one's position on these issues, it is clear that the policy debate, both in the United States and in Australia, has not been well informed by research, and different leg-

Proponents of medicinal marijuana use demonstrate at a rally hoping to change Americans' attitudes toward the herb.

islative approaches have been introduced in different locations at different times, with little or no planning for evaluating the impacts of the changes and monitoring them on an ongoing basis. Both sides of the debate have presumed that certain impacts will result from changes in policy, with little or no reference to empirical evidence.

Attitudes about and use of marijuana need to be monitored as medical use becomes more prevalent as a result of policy changes. Though the data reported here do not indicate great cause for concern, the effects of these policy changes may not be immediate. Medical legalization could, for example, lead to increased access to and availability of marijuana and this may have an effect on prevalence of use. Results from all such studies will be of interest to policy makers, researchers and public health professionals. As states legalize medical marijuana use, it will be critical to understand the impact of such policies on substance use and abuse.

SEVEN

The Federal Government Should Ban Medical Marijuana

Mark E. Souder

In the days before the creation of the Food and Drug Administration (FDA), medical fraud and quackery were rampant. Desperate for a cure for their ailments, Americans would use just about anything—even substances that were later found to be harmful. As Representative Mark E. Souder of Indiana describes in this selection, the Food and Drug Act was enacted to protect Americans from medical quackery by requiring all potential drugs to pass through rigorous clinical tests and trials before being approved for public consumption. The latest quackery to face the American public is medical marijuana, he argues. Although marijuana has never been determined to be safe as a medicine, he notes, proponents of medical marijuana have attempted to bypass FDA scrutiny by relying on state laws and voter referenda to approve marijuana for medical purposes. However, marijuana is not a medicine, Souder insists, and the Supreme Court was correct to rule against the medical marijuana proponents in *Gonzales v. Raich*. Souder is chairman of the House Government Reform Committee Subcommittee on Criminal Justice, Drug Policy, and Human Resources. He is also cochairman of the Speaker's Drug Task Force. Along with six other members of Congress, he submitted an amicus brief in the case of *Gonzales v. Raich*.

Mark E. Souder, "Marijuana Not a Medicine," *The Washington Times*, June 9, 2005, copyright © 2005 Washington Times. Reproduced by permission of the author.

In the 1890s, the Carbolic Smoke Ball Co. of Great Britain promised that its product—a substance that consumers were instructed to smoke three times each day—would cure everything, from asthma to influenza to whooping cough. Carbolic smoke balls became widely popular, especially as a "treatment" for influenza. The company's fortunes declined only when one fastidious smoke ball user contracted influenza and sued the Carbolic Smoke Ball Co., which had guaranteed that the "medicine" would protect against this epidemic.

Today, we laugh at the quack medicine that led Victorians to perch over carbolic smoke balls, hoping to cure asthma or other ailments by inhaling the smoke. And we shake our heads when we read about how cocaine was similarly abused here in the United States in the name of medicine. But the lure of quackery never diminishes.

Schorr, New York Daily News, United Features Sydicate. reproduced by permission.

"SMOKE TWO JOINTS AND CALL ME IN THE MORNING..."

The Federal Government Should Ban Medical Marijuana 59

On Monday [June 6, 2005], the Supreme Court ruled against the "medical" marijuana proponents in *Gonzales v. Raich*, a case that endeavored to return the United States to 19th-century medicine by legalizing "medical" marijuana.

"Medical" marijuana is a myth, no less so than carbolic smoke balls. Marijuana is no more a medicine than cocaine. Like any complex compound, marijuana is composed of hundreds of chemicals, and indeed some of them may, on their own, have medicinal effects. But the same could be said of virtually any substance.

Opium poppy provides real medical derivatives, such as morphine, but that doesn't mean that the ill should start using—and abusing—heroin. Indeed, medicinal derivatives of the marijuana plant—Marinol, for example, which contains synthetic THC—already exist, and have been approved by the Food and Drug Administration [FDA].

Federal Oversight Is Essential

The FDA was created precisely to combat the medical fraud and quackery that led to the phony medicines of the late 19th and early 20th centuries. In the decades since enactment of the Food and Drug Act, a regulatory system has been developed to protect the public health by ensuring the integrity of medicine. To be approved by the FDA, a drug must be proven to be safe and effective through a wide range of scientific tests, including rigorous clinical trials by the best scientists in the nation. Only then does the FDA allow a new drug to be sold to patients.

The FDA's excellent scientists have never determined that smoked marijuana is safe and effective. That is an obstacle that the pro-marijuana forces would like to remove, which is why *Gonzales v. Raich* sought to make our federal drug-approval process subservient to state referenda. If the FDA is going to stop quackery, after all, the quacks need to stop the FDA.

The ultimate goal, of course, is the legalization of marijuana—the "medical" marijuana movement is simply a means to that end. Survey data clearly demonstrate that "medical" marijuana is largely being used for recreational or emotional reasons rather than medical purposes. In Oregon, for example, Dr. Phillip E. Leveque, a pro-marijuana activist and physician, has personally written prescriptions for more than 4,000 people to use marijuana over the last several years. His license to practice medicine was finally suspended in March 2004 by the Oregon Board of Medical Examiners for his failure to provide proper examinations or oversight of this "treatment."

The consequences of this kind of quackery are real and tragic. [In 2004] 14-year-old Irma Perez was laid to rest in [Belmont,] California after dying from an ecstasy overdose at a party. Her friends, having recognized that Irma felt unwell after taking the MDMA pill, attempted to give her marijuana because they believed "that drug is sometimes used to treat cancer patients." Had she received early—and real—treatment, Irma likely would have survived the overdose.

The Supreme Court has taken a step toward ensuring that more Irmas aren't given carbolic smoke balls in their time of need.

EIGHT

The Federal Government Should Not Regulate Medical Marijuana

Julie M. Carpenter

In the next selection Julie M. Carpenter writes that the core issue in *Gonzales v. Raich* is whether the federal government has the right to override state laws. Under California law, Angel McClary Raich's physician is legally allowed to prescribe medical marijuana to his patient; under federal law, he is not. The question the Court has to decide is whether an individual patient who grows marijuana for his or her own medical purposes is violating the Commerce Clause of the Constitution. The federal government is relying on precedent. In a 1942 case, the Supreme Court decided in *Wickard v. Filburn* that under the Commerce Clause the government could regulate wheat grown by plaintiff Roscoe Filburn on his farm. However, *Gonzales v. Raich* is different. While Filburn did produce wheat for commercial purposes, Raich does not buy or sell her marijuana, and marijuana that she grows never crosses state lines. Her actions, therefore, do not violate federal law. Carpenter represented the California Nurses Association in an amicus brief filed with the Supreme Court in support of Angel McClary Raich in the case of *Gonzales v. Raich*. She is a partner in Jenner & Block's Washington, D.C., law office.

Julie M. Carpenter, "Yes, Federal Power Is Limited," *Legal Times*, November 29, 2004. Reproduced by permission.

A ngel McClary Raich had dwindled to 93 pounds after years
of medical treatment. She was confined to a wheelchair with
chronic pain. In some desperation, she began using marijuana on
her doctor's advice. Her doctor says that she has tried all other
alternatives; either they don't work, or the side effects are worse
than her symptoms.

*A gaunt Angel Raich is helped into court during her
lawsuit against the U.S. attorney general for arresting her
and others who use marijuana medicinally.*

It's her doctor's undisputed opinion that without marijuana, Raich may die. With it, she is out of the wheelchair, managing her pain, and keeping her weight up by keeping her food and medications down.

California law allows her to grow and possess medical cannabis on her doctor's advice. Federal law says she is committing a crime. Who wins this tug of war?

The Supreme Court will hear oral argument on Nov. 29 [2004] in *Ashcroft v. Raich* [in *Gonzales v. Raich* (2005), the Supreme Court ruled that the federal government can outlaw medical marijuana], the injunctive action Raich and others brought to avoid federal drug enforcement against them.

Cannot Regulate Everything

Unlike the states, Congress does not have the power to directly regulate public welfare, including the practice of medicine. In *United States v. Lopez* (1995) and *United States v. Morrison* (2000), the Supreme Court emphasized that the Constitution "withhold[s] from Congress a plenary police power that would authorize enactment of every type of legislation." It confirmed that Congress may not use a "relatively trivial impact on commerce as an excuse for broad general regulation of state or private activities." (In those cases, the Court concluded that Congress could not prohibit possession of a gun near a school or criminalize gender-based violence.)

Yet the Drug Enforcement Administration [DEA] argues that Congress' national power over interstate commerce allows it to prohibit local California patients from possessing their own state-authorized medicine in California.

Raich's medical cannabis has never entered commerce, interstate or otherwise. Two caregivers grow it in California solely for her medical use there. The marijuana is never sold, bartered, or otherwise exchanged, and it never crosses state lines. Can Congress really regulate, as interstate commerce, this kind of intrastate, noneconomic, medical possession?

The DEA says yes, because the "aggregate effect" of sick patients growing their own marijuana "substantially affects" interstate com-

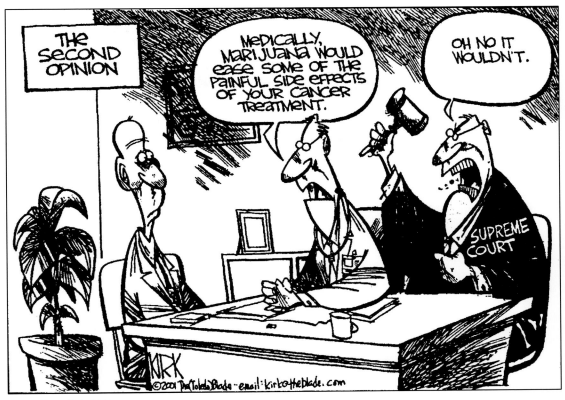

Funny Times / July 2001

merce. It relies heavily on [the Supreme Court's decision in] *Wickard v. Filburn* (1942), in which the Court held that federal wheat limits applied to wheat used entirely on the grower's farm.

But that case was inherently economic. Roscoe Filburn planted wheat as a business, producing and selling about 6.6 tons a year. An additional six tons he planted beyond his government allotment were also business-related, since he would otherwise have had to purchase those six tons from others to feed his cattle and poultry and to reseed the following year. Thus, the use of the wheat was commercial, not personal.

Here, like the student possessing a gun near a school in *Lopez*, sick patients possessing their own home-grown cannabis for their own medical use aren't engaged in any economic or commercial activity. They are not buying, selling, or exchanging; their marijuana cannot substitute for other marijuana. In short, under

California law, a sick patient grows and possesses his own cannabis outside any market.

Because the activity here is noneconomic, Supreme Court precedent does not allow Congress to aggregate the effects of that activity to somehow find an effect on interstate commerce. If Congress could do that, virtually any activity could be federally regulated.

More than the Feds

Justice Louis Brandeis famously observed. "It is one of the happy incidents of the federal system that a single courageous state may, if its citizens choose, serve as a laboratory; and try novel social and economic experiments without risk to the rest of the country."

Ten states (including Montana, whose voters just re-elected George W. Bush with 59 percent of the vote and approved medical cannabis with 62 percent) have chosen to weigh the risk of abuse versus the therapeutic benefits of cannabis differently from the DEA. This experiment, limited to the states that have chosen it, presents no risk to other states. And it presents no risk to interstate commerce, since Congress remains free to regulate marijuana actually involved in interstate commerce.

The DEA's disdain for state disagreement about medical cannabis suggests strongly that it cares less about ensuring the smooth course of commerce among the states and more about insisting that its view of medical practice—no marijuana ever—prevails.

Interestingly, other federal entities disagree. The congressionally chartered Institute of Medicine has concluded that "there are some limited circumstances in which we recommend smoking marijuana for medical purposes." And for 30 years the federal government has provided medical cannabis to a limited group of patients under an investigational new-drug compassionate-use program.

So the dispute is not really about whether marijuana has any medical value. It is about who decides whether patients can use it. To be true to the principles of federalism adopted in the

Constitution, Congress should not, in the name of administrative and prosecutorial convenience, usurp this state authority.

Finally, whatever the Court decides about the commerce clause is not the end of this case. The plaintiffs have also argued, with substantial support from the medical community, that they have a fundamental liberty interest in protecting their lives and avoiding unnecessary suffering.

If that due process right is recognized (and at least five members of the current Court have indicated it may well be), then neither state nor federal law may prohibit patients from using medical cannabis necessary to protect their health and lives. If so, Raich would still receive the medical treatment her doctor prescribed and perhaps avoid returning to her wheelchair.

NINE

Underage Patients Should Be Allowed to Use Medical Marijuana

Hastings Center Report and Kevin O'Brien

In this selection, published by the Hastings Center, the authors describe the case of JJ, a seven-year-old boy who suffers from several emotional and behavioral disorders. When all other medical treatments failed, JJ's mother, under the guidance of caseworkers and physicians, elected to take advantage of California's Compassionate Use Act of 1996 and permit her son to ingest small amounts of marijuana. Though the treatment resulted in dramatic improvements in JJ's behavior, county social workers attempted to remove JJ from his mother's care. This case study raises the moral and ethical question of whether parents have the right, under a qualified pediatrician's supervision, to administer medical marijuana to their children and whether the government should interfere in this decision. In his commentary, Kevin O'Brien insists that this case is not about an irresponsible parent looking for easy answers. It is about a concerned parent trying to help her child with a severe behavioral disorder and about a child whose treatment is being closely monitored by qualified professionals. Therefore, he concludes, the facts of this case appear to justify the decision by JJ's mother and pediatrician to administer medical marijuana. The *Hastings Center Report* is a quarterly journal published

Kevin O'Brien, "Mother and Son: The Case of Medical Marijuana (Case Study)," *The Hastings Center Report*, Vol. 32, September/October, 2002, copyright © 2002 Hastings Center. Reproduced by permission.

by the Hastings Center, an organization that is dedicated to research and studies in biomedical ethics. Privately funded through donations, the Hastings Center staff attempts to examine and resolve difficult moral and ethical issues related to health care and medicine. Its members consist of physicians, scientists, lawyers, corporate executives, and government officials. O'Brien teaches introductory courses in philosophy and ethics at Saint Joseph's University in Philadelphia, where he is a visiting instructor of philosophy.

Case Study Background

JJ is a seven-year-old boy who lives with his biological mother in California. JJ has been hyperactive and aggressive for most of his life. He says he has bad thoughts and that he hears voices telling him to kill his mother. He has been diagnosed with post-traumatic stress disorder, bipolar disorder, and impulse control disorder.

The many forms of ingesting marijuana are displayed in this cannabis club offering of various cakes and cookies as well as smokeable herb.

In the past four years he has seen sixteen physicians, who have prescribed over nineteen medications—ritalin, dexedrine, adderall, depakote, imipramine, clonidine, thioridazine, guanfacine, tegretol, and others. Often, he has been overmedicated, to the point of slobbering, slurring his words, and being unable to walk. He has been hospitalized three times at a psychiatric hospital and has been asked to leave eight preschools. His mother has pursued all forms of medical help, from medications to behavior modification. She has tried spanking/not spanking, a "holding" technique that made her son even more violent, single medications, multiple medications, constantly increased dosages, and numerous care treatment options. She has on several occasions questioned the wisdom of all the medications, and she has worked with his various physicians to remove JJ from the ineffective medications as it became evident that none of them were helping. She believed that many of his symptoms may have resulted from the side effects of the medications and not the underlying behavior.

© 2004, Tribune Media, South Florida Sun Sentinel. Used by permission.

The physicians at the psychiatric hospital believed that JJ appeared better when the medications were stopped and he was placed in a strictly structured environment.

In May of 2001, when it appeared that JJ was about to enter yet another round of medication, his mother discovered in the course of her research that medical marijuana might help her son. She knew nothing about the medical use of marijuana and did not support the current movement in California. However, she discussed the option with caseworkers, team members, and several physicians. After consulting with them, she decided to give the treatment a try. She notified JJ's medical team that he was no longer on any psychotropic medications and had begun treatment with medical marijuana, as outlined under California's Proposition 215, or the Compassionate Use Act of 1996. Currently, JJ takes the marijuana in a muffin—one half of a muffin (containing one-forty-eighth of a cup of pulverized dry leaves) in the morning, and one half in the afternoon. JJ is monitored by a pediatrician, who adjusts the dosage.

Positive Results

The results have been very good. JJ's social worker and teachers report that his behavior has taken a dramatic turn. His demeanor is very polite and he interacts enthusiastically with staff and students. The most noticeable change is JJ's ability to use words: now, when he becomes frustrated in class, he explains what the problem is and he is no longer afraid to get help from the staff. He has also become more willing to help others who function at a lower academic level. His mother acknowledges that it is too early to say what the long-term effects will be, and she says she will discontinue the medication if it no longer appears to be helping him.

When county officials heard that JJ's mother was allowing him to use medical marijuana, they immediately tried to remove JJ from his mother's care. JJ's mother sought legal assistance and has been able to keep custody of JJ. But the question remains: do parents have the right to allow their children to use medical marijuana, and do physicians have the prerogative to prescribe it in such situations?

Kevin O'Brien's Commentary

This case concerns two kinds of relationships long protected under the law: that between parent and child and that between physician and patient. Inherent in both relationships is that the first member of each pair bears a duty to serve the best interests of the other. For the parent, that duty is rooted in the natural bond between parent and child. Courts recognize that the parent is usually in the best position to care for the child. For the physician, the duty derives from the nature of the medical profession itself: physicians must try to help their patients get better. To protect and support these relationships, which are fundamental to a well-ordered society, courts and legislatures have established a wide array of privileges, rights, and responsibilities for parents and physicians. The government suspends or overrides these protections and supports only where the best interests of the child or patient are not being served, or where there is some compelling societal interest at stake. The presumption, both moral and legal, favors the parent and physician.

The primary responsibility for JJ lies with his mother. Both law and morality respect the autonomy of parents to determine medical care for children. For this case, the state law is clear: California's Compassionate Use Act of 1996 allows a primary caregiver, such as JJ's mother, to use marijuana to treat any illness for which the drug can provide relief. The moral question is more complicated: Reading the facts, our natural sympathies lie with the mother, who has seen her son endure countless therapies to treat his disorders over seven years. With medicinal marijuana, she found a medication that works with dramatic results. JJ functions much better, both academically and socially, and can rid himself of a medley of medications that may have only exacerbated his condition. The mother's decision to use medicinal marijuana was well researched, and JJ is under the supervision of physicians.

This is not the case of someone seeking a quick fix or an easy way out. This case is about a caring, prudent mother who wants to do what is best for her child. The long-term effects are admittedly unclear, but JJ's mother is prepared to discontinue the treatment if the medicine is no longer helping him. While at first we

A physician (right) in Oregon, where medicinal use of marijuana is legal, interviews a patient about the possibility of using marijuana for treatment.

may hesitate, as JJ's mother did, in approving the use of medical marijuana, in this case it is the morally responsible action for the mother to take.

The Pediatrician's Duty

As for JJ's pediatrician, we must look to the ethical norms of the medical profession for guidance. Physicians must above all do no harm, and according to the principle of beneficence, they must care for the well-being of their patients. JJ's pediatrician has a right and a duty at least to inform the mother about medicinal marijuana as an option and explain to her the foreseeable risks and benefits. The facts clearly indicate that medicinal marijuana is helping JJ. There may be risks in taking marijuana, but there are risks associated with any medicine. JJ used a variety of other medications that caused harmful side effects; so far, he has not experienced similar effects with medicinal marijuana. If the harm to JJ's short-term or long-term health becomes clear, both the pediatrician and his mother would be obligated to stop administering the medicinal marijuana to JJ.

While the relationship between a parent and child and a physician and patient is privileged, the government may interfere in these relationships for compelling reasons. In this case, the government's interests are varied. While permitting marijuana to be used for research purposes, the federal government has routinely objected to legalizing marijuana for medicinal purposes. It contends that the drug is harmful to the user's health, addictive when used, and likely to lead to more serious drug use. The government also contends that allowing marijuana for medicinal purposes will send the message, especially to children, that marijuana is acceptable to use recreationally and may even be good for you.

While the federal government's concerns are reasonable, they are far from conclusive in this case. Whether JJ will become addicted to marijuana or suffer harmful long-term effects is uncertain. The claim that he is more likely to do more serious drugs recreationally is equally unclear. His mother is giving him small doses of marijuana daily, under the supervision of a physician and under the sanction of state law. That other children will get the "wrong idea" about marijuana use from JJ's use is highly debatable. JJ's mother gives her son marijuana to help him with a severe behavioral disorder, and his use of marijuana is strictly monitored by adults. This is not the case of a minor who smokes pot recreationally, far from public view. The message here is that marijuana, like other drugs, is a medication that must be carefully and responsibly administered, not abused. The physician's and mother's right to provide the marijuana to JJ should not be curtailed by the federal government's attempt—however noble—to make "zero tolerance" the law of the land.

To defend the use of marijuana on the specific facts of JJ's case is not, of course, to approve the use of marijuana in all medical cases, and especially not to approve its recreational use. But in this case, for government officials to interfere with the mother's and the pediatrician's ethically responsible decision will only undercut JJ's best interests, which the government too seeks to promote.

TEN

Marijuana Should Be Legalized for Medical and Recreational Purposes

Ethan A. Nadelmann

While many Americans favor the idea of decriminalizing and even legalizing marijuana, even more Americans support making marijuana legal for medical purposes. As Ethan A. Nadelmann writes in this selection, state ballots to legalize medical marijuana typically have overwhelming public support. Nevertheless, federal laws prohibit marijuana use. Approximately seven hundred thousand people are arrested per year for marijuana offenses, the vast majority of them for possession of small amounts of marijuana. Costs for enforcing marijuana laws have reached the billions. Like all psychoactive drugs, marijuana does have its problems. However, Nadelmann contends the federal government is overreacting to these problems. Marijuana is no more dangerous or addictive than other drugs that are legal, he argues, and the medicinal benefit of marijuana is no longer disputed. He concludes that just like alcohol prohibition in the 1920s, marijuana prohibition is costly and counterproductive and should be ended. Nadelmann is the founder and executive director of Drug Policy Alliance, the leading organization in the United States promoting alternatives to the war on drugs.

Ethan A. Nadelmann, "An End to Prohibition," *National Review*, July 12, 2004, copyright © 2004 by National Review, Inc., 251 Lexington Avenue, New York, NY 10016. Reproduced by permission.

Never before have so many Americans supported decriminalizing and even legalizing marijuana. Seventy-two percent say that for simple marijuana possession, people should not be incarcerated but fined: the generally accepted definition of "decriminalization." Even more Americans support making marijuana legal for medical purposes. Support for broader legalization ranges between 25 and 42 percent, depending on how one asks the question. Two of every five Americans—according to a 2003 Zogby poll—say "the government should treat marijuana more or less the same way it treats alcohol: It should regulate it, control it, tax it, and only make it illegal for children."

Close to 100 million Americans—including more than half of those between the ages of 18 and 50—have tried marijuana at

Young people at a 1967 gathering in a park pass around a pot pipe, the smoking of which at that time was often an act of youthful rebellion.

least once. Military and police recruiters often have no choice but to ignore past marijuana use by job seekers. The public apparently feels the same way about presidential and other political candidates. Al Gore, Bill Bradley, and John Kerry all say they smoked pot in days past. So did Bill Clinton, with his notorious caveat. George W. Bush won't deny he did. And ever more political, business, religious, intellectual, and other leaders plead guilty as well.

The debate over ending marijuana prohibition simmers just below the surface of mainstream politics, crossing ideological and partisan boundaries. Marijuana is no longer the symbol of Sixties rebellion and Seventies permissiveness, and it's not just liberals and libertarians who say it should be legal, as [conservative syndicated columnist] William F. Buckley Jr. has demonstrated better than anyone. As director of the country's leading drug-policy-reform organization, I've had countless conversations with police and prosecutors, judges and politicians, and hundreds of others who quietly agree that the criminalization of marijuana is costly, foolish, and destructive. What's most needed now is principled conservative leadership. Buckley has led the way, and New Mexico's former governor, Gary Johnson, spoke out courageously while in office. How about others?

A Systemic Overreaction to Marijuana Offenses

Marijuana prohibition is unique among American criminal laws. No other law is both enforced so widely and harshly and yet deemed unnecessary by such a substantial portion of the populace.

Police make about 700,000 arrests per year for marijuana offenses. That's almost the same number as are arrested each year for cocaine, heroin, methamphetamine, Ecstasy, and all other illicit drugs combined. Roughly 600,000, or 87 percent, of marijuana arrests are for nothing more than possession of small amounts. Millions of Americans have never been arrested or convicted of any criminal offense except this. Enforcing marijuana laws costs an estimated $10–15 billion in direct costs alone.

Punishments range widely across the country, from modest fines to a few days in jail to many years in prison. Prosecutors often contend that no one goes to prison for simple possession, but tens, perhaps hundreds, of thousands of people on probation and parole are locked up each year because their urine tested positive for marijuana or because they were picked up in possession of a joint. Alabama currently locks up people convicted three times of marijuana possession for 15 years to life. There are probably no firm estimates [that] exist—100,000 Americans behind bars tonight for one marijuana offense or another. And even for those who don't lose their freedom, simply being arrested can be traumatic and costly. A parent's marijuana use can be the basis for taking away her children and putting them in foster care. Foreign-born residents of the U.S. can be deported for a marijuana offense no matter how long they have lived in this country, no matter if their children are U.S. citizens, and no matter how long they have been legally employed. More than half the states revoke or suspend driver's licenses of people arrested for marijuana possession even though they were not driving at the time of arrest. The federal Higher Education Act prohibits student loans to young people convicted of any drug offense; all other criminal offenders remain eligible.

This is clearly an overreaction on the part of government. No drug is perfectly safe, and every psychoactive drug can be used in ways that are problematic. The federal government has spent billions of dollars on advertisements and anti-drug programs that preach the dangers of marijuana—that it's a gateway drug, and addictive in its own right, and dramatically more potent than it used to be, and responsible for all sorts of physical and social diseases as well as international terrorism. But the government has yet to repudiate the 1988 finding of the Drug Enforcement Administration's own administrative law judge, Francis Young, who concluded after extensive testimony that "marijuana in its natural form is one of the safest therapeutically active substances known to man."

Misleading Warnings

Is marijuana a gateway drug? Yes, insofar as most Americans try marijuana before they try other illicit drugs. But no, insofar as the

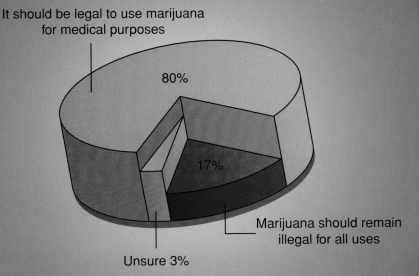

It should be legal to use marijuana
for medical purposes

80%

17%

Marijuana should remain
illegal for all uses

Unsure 3%

Source: NORML

vast majority of Americans who have tried marijuana have never gone on to try other illegal drugs, much less get in trouble with them, and most have never even gone on to become regular or problem marijuana users. Trying to reduce heroin addiction by preventing marijuana use, it's been said, is like trying to reduce motorcycle fatalities by cracking down on bicycle riding. If marijuana did not exist, there's little reason to believe that there would be less drug abuse in the U.S.; indeed, its role would most likely be filled by a more dangerous substance.

Is marijuana dramatically more potent today? There's certainly a greater variety of high-quality marijuana available today than 30 years ago. But anyone who smoked marijuana in the 1970s and 1980s can recall smoking pot that was just as strong as anything available today. What's more, one needs to take only a few puffs of higher-potency pot to get the desired effect, so there's less wear and tear on the lungs.

Is marijuana addictive? Yes, it can be, in that some people use it to excess, in ways that are problematic for themselves and those around them, and find it hard to stop. But marijuana may well be the least addictive and least damaging of all commonly used psychoactive drugs, including many that are now legal. Most people who smoke marijuana never become dependent. Withdrawal symptoms pale compared with those from other drugs. No one has ever died from a marijuana overdose, which cannot be said of most other drugs. Marijuana is not associated with violent behavior and only minimally with reckless sexual behavior. And even heavy marijuana smokers smoke only a fraction of what cigarette addicts smoke. Lung cancers involving only marijuana are rare.

A youthful prison inmate attends a drug treatment session, which is often mandated by the state as part of the penalty for drug-possession convictions.

The government's most recent claim is that marijuana abuse accounts for more people entering treatment than any other illegal drug. That shouldn't be surprising, given that tens of millions of Americans smoke marijuana while only a few million use all other illicit drugs. But the claim is spurious nonetheless. Few Americans who enter "treatment" for marijuana are addicted. Fewer than one in five people entering drug treatment for marijuana do so voluntarily. More than half were referred by the criminal-justice system. They go because they got caught with a joint or failed a drug test at school or work (typically for having smoked marijuana days ago, not for being impaired), or because they were caught by a law-enforcement officer—and attending a marijuana "treatment" program is what's required to avoid expulsion, dismissal, or incarceration. Many traditional drug-treatment programs shamelessly participate in this charade to preserve a profitable and captive client stream.

Even those who recoil at the "nanny state" telling adults what they can or cannot sell to one another, often make an exception when it comes to marijuana—to "protect the kids." This is a bad joke, as any teenager will attest. The criminalization of marijuana for adults has not prevented young people from having better access to marijuana than anyone else. Even as marijuana's popularity has waxed and waned since the 1970s, one statistic has remained constant: More than 80 percent of high-school students report it's easy to get. Meanwhile, the government's exaggerations and outright dishonesty easily backfire. For every teen who refrains from trying marijuana because it's illegal (for adults), another is tempted by its status as "forbidden fruit." Many respond to the lies about marijuana by disbelieving warnings about more dangerous drugs. So much for protecting the kids by criminalizing the adults.

The Medical Dimension

The debate over medical marijuana obviously colors the broader debate over marijuana prohibition. Marijuana's medical efficacy is no longer in serious dispute. Its use as a medicine dates back thousands of years. Pharmaceutical products containing marijuana's

Angel Raich, a medical marijuana user, demonstrates the use of a marijuana vaporizer, a nonsmoking form of ingesting cannabis.

central ingredient, THC, are legally sold in the U.S., and more are emerging. Some people find the pill form satisfactory, and others consume it in teas or baked products. Most find smoking the easiest and most effective way to consume this unusual medicine, but non-smoking consumption methods, notably vaporizers, are emerging.

Federal law still prohibits medical marijuana. But every state ballot initiative to legalize medical marijuana has been approved, often by wide margins—in California, Washington, Oregon, Alaska, Colorado, Nevada, Maine, and Washington, D.C. State legislatures in Vermont, Hawaii, and Maryland have followed suit, and many others are now considering their own medical-marijuana bills—including New York, Connecticut, Rhode Island, and Illinois. Support is often bipartisan, with Republican governors like Gary Johnson and Maryland's Bob Ehrlich taking the lead. In New York's 2002 gubernatorial campaign, the conservative candidate of the

Independence party, Tom Golisano, surprised everyone by campaigning heavily on this issue. The medical-marijuana bill now before the New York legislature is backed not just by leading Republicans but even by some Conservative party leaders.

The political battleground increasingly pits the White House—first under Clinton and now Bush—against everyone else. Majorities in virtually every state in the country would vote, if given the chance, to legalize medical marijuana. Even Congress is beginning to turn; [in 2003] about two-thirds of House Democrats and a dozen Republicans voted in favor of an amendment co-sponsored by Republican Dana Rohrabacher to prohibit federal funding of any Justice Department crackdowns on medical marijuana in the states that had legalized it. (Many more Republicans privately expressed support, but were directed to vote against.) And federal courts have imposed limits on federal aggression: first in *Conant v. Walters*, which now protects the First Amendment rights of doctors and patients to discuss medical marijuana, and more recently in *Raich v. Ashcroft* and *Santa Cruz v. Ashcroft*, which determined that the federal government's power to regulate interstate commerce does not provide a basis for prohibiting medical-marijuana operations that are entirely local and non-commercial.

States Becoming Increasingly Involved

State and local governments are increasingly involved in trying to regulate medical marijuana, notwithstanding the federal prohibition. California, Oregon, Hawaii, Alaska, Colorado, and Nevada have created confidential medical-marijuana patient registries, which protect bona fide patients and caregivers from arrest or prosecution. Some municipal governments are now trying to figure out how to regulate production and distribution. In California, where dozens of medical-marijuana programs now operate openly, with tacit approval by local authorities, some program directors are asking to be licensed and regulated. Many state and local authorities, including law enforcement, favor this but are intimidated by federal threats to arrest and prosecute them for violating federal law.

The drug czar and DEA spokespersons recite the mantra that "there is no such thing as medical marijuana," but the claim is so specious on its face that it clearly undermines federal credibility. The federal government currently provides marijuana—from its own production site in Mississippi—to a few patients who years ago were recognized by the courts as bona fide patients. No one wants to debate those who have used marijuana for medical purposes, be it Santa Cruz medical-marijuana hospice founder Valerie Corral or *National Review*'s Richard Brookhiser. Even many federal officials quietly regret the assault on medical marijuana. When the DEA raided Corral's hospice in September 2002, one agent was heard to say, "Maybe I'm going to think about getting another job sometime soon."

The Broader Movement

The bigger battle, of course, concerns whether marijuana prohibition will ultimately go the way of alcohol Prohibition, replaced by a variety of state and local tax and regulatory policies with modest federal involvement. Dedicated prohibitionists see medical marijuana as the first step down a slippery slope to full legalization. The voters who approved the medical-marijuana ballot initiatives (as well as the wealthy men who helped fund the campaigns) were roughly divided between those who support broader legalization and those who don't, but united in seeing the criminalization and persecution of medical-marijuana patients as the most distasteful aspect of the war on marijuana.

The medical-marijuana effort has probably aided the broader anti-prohibitionist campaign in three ways. It helped transform the face of marijuana in the media, from the stereotypical rebel with long hair and tie-dyed shirt to an ordinary middle-aged American struggling with MS [multiple sclerosis] or cancer or AIDS. By winning first Proposition 215, the 1996 medical-marijuana ballot initiative in California, and then a string of similar victories in other states, the nascent drug-policy-reform movement demonstrated that it could win in the big leagues of American politics. And the emergence of successful models of medical-marijuana control is likely to boost public confidence in the possibilities and virtue of regulating nonmedical use as well.

In this regard, the history of Dutch policy on cannabis (i.e., marijuana and hashish) is instructive. The "coffee shop" model in the Netherlands, where retail (but not wholesale) sale of cannabis is de facto legal, was not legislated into existence. It evolved in fits and starts following the decriminalization of cannabis by Parliament in 1976, as consumers, growers, and entrepreneurs negotiated and collaborated with local police, prosecutors, and other authorities to find an acceptable middle-ground policy. "Coffee shops" now operate throughout the country, subject to local regulations.

Patrons of one of numerous Dutch cannabis cafés line up for their turn to take a hit from a bong.

Troublesome shops are shut down, and most are well integrated into local city cultures. Cannabis is no more popular than in the U.S. and other Western countries, notwithstanding the effective absence of criminal sanctions and controls. Parallel developments are now underway in other countries.

Like the Dutch decriminalization law in 1976, California's Prop 215 in 1996 initiated a dialogue over how best to implement the new law. The variety of outlets that have emerged—ranging from pharmacy-like stores to medical "coffee shops" to hospices, all of which provide marijuana only to people with a patient ID card or doctor's recommendation—play a key role as the most public symbol and manifestation of this dialogue. More such outlets will likely pop up around the country as other states legalize marijuana for medical purposes and then seek ways to regulate distribution and access. And the question will inevitably arise: If the emerging system is successful in controlling production and distribution of marijuana for those with a medical need, can it not also expand to provide for those without medical need?

The "Aspirin" of the 21st Century?

Millions of Americans use marijuana not just "for fun" but because they find it useful for many of the same reasons that people drink alcohol or take pharmaceutical drugs. It's akin to the beer, glass of wine, or cocktail at the end of the workday, or the prescribed drug to alleviate depression or anxiety, or the sleeping pill, or the aid to sexual function and pleasure. More and more Americans are apt to describe some or all of their marijuana use as "medical" as the definition of that term evolves and broadens. Their anecdotal experiences are increasingly backed by new scientific research into marijuana's essential ingredients, the cannabinoids. Last year [2003], a subsidiary of *The Lancet*, Britain's leading medical journal, speculated whether marijuana might soon emerge as the "aspirin of the 21st century," providing a wide array of medical benefits at low cost to diverse populations.

Perhaps the expansion of the medical-control model provides the best answer—at least in the U.S.—to the question of how best to reduce the substantial costs and harms of marijuana prohibition without inviting significant increases in real drug abuse. It's analogous to the evolution of many pharmaceutical drugs from prescription to over-the-counter, but with stricter controls still in place. It's also an incrementalist approach to reform that can provide both the control and the reassurance that cautious politicians and voters desire.

In 1931, with public support for alcohol Prohibition rapidly waning, President [Herbert] Hoover released the report of the Wickersham Commission. The report included a devastating critique of Prohibition's failures and costly consequences, but the commissioners, apparently fearful of getting out too far ahead of public opinion, opposed repeal. . . .

Two years later, federal alcohol Prohibition was history.

What support there is for marijuana prohibition would likely end quickly absent the billions of dollars spent annually by federal and other governments to prop it up. All those anti-marijuana ads pretend to be about reducing drug abuse, but in fact their basic purpose is sustaining popular support for the war on marijuana. What's needed now are conservative politicians willing to say enough is enough: Tens of billions of taxpayer dollars down the drain each year. People losing their jobs, their property, and their freedom for nothing more than possessing a joint or growing a few marijuana plants. And all for what? To send a message? To keep pretending that we're protecting our children? Alcohol Prohibition made a lot more sense than marijuana prohibition does today and it, too, was a disaster.

What You Should Know About Medical Marijuana

Facts About Marijuana

- In addition to its main active ingredient, delta-9-tetrahydrocannabinol (THC), marijuana contains more than 400 known chemicals.
- A single marijuana cigarette contains four times as much cancer-causing tar as a filtered cigarette.
- Approximately 2.4 million Americans used marijuana for the first time in 2000.
- The estimated number of Americans who used marijuana for the first time during the previous year increased from 1.4 million in 1990 to 2.5 million in 1996.
- In 2002 over 14 million Americans age 12 and older used marijuana at least once in the month prior to being surveyed.
- About one in six 10th-graders and nearly one in four high school seniors report they are current marijuana users (that is, used marijuana within the past month).
- In 1999 more than 220,000 people entered publicly funded drug treatment programs for primary marijuana abuse.
- In 2002 nearly 120,000 people were admitted to emergency rooms suffering from marijuana-related problems.
- Marijuana is the most commonly used illicit drug (used by 76 percent of current illicit drug users).

Facts About Marijuana Prohibition

- Between 95 and 100 million Americans admit to having tried marijuana, and about 14.5 million say they use it at least monthly.
- Approximately 7 million marijuana arrests have been made in the United States since 1995, including 771,984 arrests in 2004.
- A marijuana-related arrest is made, on average, every 41 seconds.
- About 89 percent of all marijuana arrests are for possession (as opposed to manufacture and/or distribution).
- Cultivation of even one marijuana plant is a federal felony.
- A minimum one-year prison sentence is mandated for "distributing" or "manufacturing" controlled substances within 1,000 feet (305m) of any school, university, or playground.

Facts About Medical Marijuana

- The federal government has designated marijuana as a Schedule I controlled substance, which means that it is deemed to have no commonly accepted medical use.
- The federal government currently allows only 7 patients in the United States to use marijuana as a medicine; the program is closed to new applicants.
- Since 1996, 11 states have legalized medical marijuana use.
- The federal government has continued to declare medical marijuana illegal even in states with laws permitting its use.
- In June 2005 the U.S. Supreme Court ruled in *Raich v. Ashcroft* that federal law overrides state law in the area of medical marijuana.
- In 1999 the Institute of Medicine reported that "cannabinoid drugs" had therapeutic value for treating pain, controlling nausea and vomiting, and stimulating the appetite, but concluded that "there is very little future in smoked marijuana as a medically approved medication."
- A synthetic version of THC in pill form called Marinol, approved by the federal Food and Drug Administration as safe and effective, has been available by prescription since 1985.

- Fifty-five percent of Americans believe possession of small amounts of marijuana should not be treated as a criminal offense.
- Seventy-eight percent of Americans support making marijuana legally available for doctors to prescribe in order to reduce pain and suffering.
- Fifty-four percent of surveyed oncologists favored the "controlled availability" of marijuana.
- Eighteen percent of surveyed pediatricians favor legalization of medical marijuana.
- Organizations that support legal access to medical marijuana include the American Bar Association, the American Academy of Family Physicians, the American Nurses Association, and the California Medical Association, to name a few (for a complete list, see www.mpp.org/mmjfacts.html).

What You Should Do About Medical Marijuana

The legalization of marijuana for medical purposes is a divisive issue that generates heated debate. On one side, proponents of legalization contend that only smoked marijuana can relieve the suffering of patients with certain medical conditions, such as glaucoma and nausea induced by chemotherapy, and that it is the duty of society to treat illness with all available means. On the other side, opponents argue that legalizing marijuana for one group only encourages more widespread and dangerous drug use and abuse, and that it is the duty of society to protect its members from harming themselves and others. Thus, both sides in the debate insist the course of action they advocate will benefit society and increase individual well-being.

How can you develop an informed opinion on this issue? How should you present well-made arguments to persuade others that your point of view is correct? Finally, what can you do to affect public policies on this subject?

Gather Information

An informed opinion on any topic depends first on knowing the facts. Do as much research as you can about marijuana in general and medical marijuana in particular. Specifically, read as much as possible about marijuana's active ingredients and their harmful and beneficial effects. Start with the essays contained in this volume. Visit your school or local library for additional resources such as books, magazine articles, and encyclopedia entries. There have been many scientific studies of the potential positive and negative effects of the drug—look for published reports in medical and science journals. If you find a full report is too long or technical, look for an abstract, or concise summary, at the beginning of the article that explains the researchers' conclusions quickly and simply.

Use Internet search engines such as Google to gather more information. Many organizations that support or oppose the legalization of marijuana (either for recreational use or medicinal use) have Web sites that offer fact sheets, position papers, and links to related resources.

It may also be possible to collect information through personal interviews. Ask someone you know who has used marijuana to describe his or her experience with the drug. If you live in a state that has legalized medical marijuana, consider calling or visiting a cannabis buyers' club to interview the staff or clients. Interview a police officer or a counselor at a drug-treatment center and get their views about marijuana and the pros and cons of legalizing it for medical use. In short, gather as much information as you can from a wide variety of sources.

Define the Debate

Once you have plenty of information, methodically review it to discover and organize the major points of contention in the debate. Who supports legalizing marijuana for medical purposes, and what are the major arguments in favor of legalization? Who opposes legalization of medical marijuana, and what are their major arguments?

You will find that the topics of medical marijuana and recreational marijuana use are closely linked. Arguments for and against medical marijuana will touch on arguments for and against recreational marijuana. For example, some opponents of legalizing medical marijuana charge that medical marijuana advocates also want to legalize marijuana for recreational purposes and are using the issue as a "Trojan Horse"—a way to sneak legalization of a dangerous drug past an unsuspecting public by presenting it as an attempt to help sick people.

Some proponents may indeed be in favor of widespread legalization of drugs. Others have narrower goals and seek simply to legalize marijuana for medical uses only. It will be necessary to

define the various positions in the debate before you begin to ana-
lyze them.

Evaluate Your Sources of Information

In forming your opinion on any topic it is important to evaluate
the sources of the information you have gathered. The authors of
books, magazine articles, newspaper editorials, government reports,
and other documents generally have a point of view, and even if
they are not frankly trying to enlist the reader's support, their personal interests or biases may be reflected in their writing. To help
you separate fact from opinion and judge the merit of a writer's
argument, consider the writer's credentials and the nature and
purposes of the organizations he or she is associated with.

For example, if you read an article by the executive director of
the National Organization for the Reform of Marijuana Laws, an
organization that advocates the legalization of marijuana, you
should expect the author to present information that emphasizes
the benefits of marijuana and omit or discount information about
harmful effects. On the other hand, a report by the federal Drug
Enforcement Administration, which opposes legalization, is likely to emphasize research that concludes marijuana is harmful and
to downplay the drug's benign or beneficial aspects.

While the information in both of these documents may be entirely valid, each author is likely to stress the facts that support his or
her views as well as those of whatever organization he or she represents. In short, rather than simply accepting all information at
face value, read critically and be aware of the biases that influence your sources.

Examine Your Values

The debate over medical marijuana often revolves around moral
values. Take some time to explore your thoughts about the morality of this issue. Those who oppose medical marijuana believe
marijuana is harmful and that it is therefore morally questionable
to legitimize its use by legalizing it. Proponents, on the other hand,

contend it is morally wrong to deprive sick people of a potentially beneficial medicine. Your opinion may ultimately depend on
your own sense of right and wrong.

Your personal experience may also affect your objectivity on
this issue. Perhaps you or someone you love has been stricken
with one of the illnesses whose symptoms marijuana is said to
relieve. This factor may make you more likely to favor the legalization of medical marijuana on emotional or moral grounds. On
the other hand, maybe you, a friend, or a family member has a
history of drug abuse or addiction. Painful personal experience
may lead you to give extra weight to research suggesting that
marijuana has dangerous addictive properties and influence you
to oppose legalization.

Examine your personal values, principles, and biases in reach-
ing a position on this issue. Do you believe it is immoral to allow
sick people to use marijuana, or immoral to deny them access to
it? You may wish to consult your parents or religious leaders for
guidance on this question.

Form an Opinion and Take Action

Once you have gathered and organized information, defined the
terms of the debate, evaluated your sources of information, and
examined your own values on the issue, you will be prepared to
take a position regarding the legalization of medical marijuana,
and to defend your opinion. You may be strongly in favor of or
strongly opposed to legalization, but remember that unqualified
support and unqualified opposition represent the most extreme
positions on the issue. Your own view may fall in-between the
extremes, reflecting compromise, support with reservations, or less
than total opposition. You may even conclude that neither side's
arguments are convincing and you cannot take a position on this
issue at the present time. In this case, however, ask yourself what
you would need to know to be able to make up your mind; perhaps
a bit more research would give you that information. Whatever
your position, make sure you can explain it reasonably, based on
facts, evidence, and thoughtfully developed beliefs.

Depending on the position you take, you may be motivated to promote it actively. Activism can take many forms. You might simply decide to educate your friends and family about medical marijuana through informal discussion. Or you might take a more systematic and formal approach. Consider joining an organization that either supports or opposes legalization of medical marijuana; most advocacy organizations' Web sites include contact information. You may also wish to make your voice heard in the political arena. Consider writing letters to your congressperson or throwing your support behind or against efforts to legalize marijuana for medical purposes in your state.

Regardless of whether or not you take action—and what type of action you take—once you have thoroughly researched the topic and examined your own values, you will be able to participate intelligently in the debate over medical marijuana. And your critical thinking skills will be sharper the next time you are called on to think about a controversial issue and decide where you stand.

American Alliance for Medical Cannabis (AAMC)
Web site: www.letfreedomgrow.com

AAMC consists of health professionals, patients, educators, clergy, caregivers, and community members, as well as experts in the field of medical cannabis. Its main mission is patient advocacy and support, although its mission also includes clinical research and education.

American Council for Drug Education (ACDE)
164 W. Seventy-fourth St.
New York, NY 10023
(800) 488-3784 or (212) 595-5810, ext. 7860
fax: (212) 595-2553
e-mail: acde@phoenixhouse.org
Web site: www.acde.org

The American Council for Drug Education informs the public about the harmful effects of abusing drugs and alcohol. It gives the public access to scientifically based prevention programs and materials. ACDE has resources for parents, youth, educators, prevention professionals, employers, health-care professionals, and other concerned community members who are working to help America's youth avoid the dangers of drug and alcohol abuse.

Americans for Safe Access (ASA)
1322 Webster St., Suite 208
Oakland, CA 94612
(510) 251-1856 or (888) 929-4367
fax: (510) 251-2036
e-mail: info@safeaccessnow.org
Web site: www.safeaccessnow.org

Americans for Safe Access is a grassroots political campaign of medical marijuana patients, doctors, caregivers, and supporters working to legalize marijuana for medical purposes. ASA uses a variety of tactics to raise awareness and demand political change, provide a range of support and resources for local activists, and organize coordinated national action.

California Cannabis Research Medical Group (CCRMG)
PO Box 9143
Berkeley, CA 94709
e-mail: contact@ccrmg.org
Web site: www.ccrmg.org

The CCRMG is dedicated to conducting quality medical cannabis research, to ensuring the safety and confidentiality of all research subjects, and to maintaining the highest quality of standards and risk management. CCRMG is involved with many projects to further promote medicinal marijuana, including the publication of O'Shaughnessy's *Journal of the California Cannabis Research Medical Group.*

Common Sense for Drug Policy (CSDP)
1377-C Spencer Ave.
Lancaster, PA 17603
(717) 299-0600
fax: (717) 393-4953
e-mail: info@csdp.org
Web site: www.csdp.org

Common Sense for Drug Policy is dedicated to reforming drug policy and expanding harm reduction. It disseminates information; comments on existing laws, policies, and practices; and provides assistance to individuals and organizations. In addition to advocating the regulation of marijuana in a manner similar to the regulation of alcohol, CSDP favors decriminalizing the use of hard drugs and providing them only through prescription.

Community Anti-Drug Coalitions of America (CADCA)
625 Slaters La., Suite 300
Alexandria, VA 22314
(800) 54-CADCA
fax: (703) 706-0565
Web site: http://cadca.org/CoalitionResources/PP-marijuana Info.asp

CADCA's mission is to create safe, healthy, drug-free communities. The organization supports its members with technical assistance and training, public policy, media strategies and marketing programs, conferences, and special events.

Drug Free America Foundation, Inc.
2600 Ninth St. N., Suite 200
St. Petersburg, FL 33704-2744
(727) 828-0211
fax: (727) 828-0212
Web site: www.dfaf.org

Drug Free America Foundation, Inc., is a drug prevention and policy organization committed to developing, promoting, and sustaining global strategies, policies, and laws that will reduce illegal drug use, drug addiction, and drug-related injuries and deaths. Its reference collection contains more than twenty-one hundred books and other media chronicling the rise of the drug culture and current drug policy issues.

Drug Prevention Network of the Americas (DPNA)
Web site: www.dpna.org

Drug Prevention Network of the Americas is a nonprofit corporation committed to the education and prevention of drug abuse in the Western Hemisphere. Its Web portal serves as a clearinghouse for the exchange of information related to drug abuse prevention, harm reduction, drug legalization, the war on drugs, and drug impact. The site provides links to prevention resources along with downloadable brochures, presentations, and technical papers.

Drug Watch International
PO Box 45218
Omaha, NE 68145-0218
(402) 384-9212
Web site: www.drugwatch.org

Drug Watch International is a volunteer nonprofit drug information network and advocacy organization that promotes the creation of healthy drug-free cultures in the world and opposes the legalization of drugs. The organization upholds a comprehensive approach to drug issues involving prevention, education, intervention/treatment, and law enforcement/interdiction. It provides policy makers, the media, and the public with current information to counter drug advocacy propaganda.

Institute for Behavior and Health
6191 Executive Blvd.
Rockville, MD 20852
(301) 231-9010
fax: (301) 770-6876
e-mail: contactus@ibhinc.org
Web site: www.ibhinc.org

The Institute for Behavior and Health creates strategies that will promote a drug-free America. These strategies include improving drug abuse treatment programs, encouraging student drug testing programs, expanding drug prevention and treatment programs in the workplace, and reducing drug abuse in the criminal justice system, among others.

Marijuana Policy Project
PO Box 77492, Capitol Hill
Washington, DC 20013
(202) 462-5747
fax: (202) 232-0442
e-mail: mpp@mpp.org
Web site: www.mpp.org

The Marijuana Policy Project develops and promotes policies to minimize the harm associated with marijuana laws. The project increases public awareness through speaking engagements, educational seminars, and the mass media. Briefing papers and news articles, as well as the quarterly *MPP Report*, can be accessed on its Web site.

National Center on Addiction and Substance Abuse (CASA)
Columbia University, 633 Third Ave., 19th Fl.
New York, NY 10017-6706
(212) 841-5200
fax: (212) 956-8020
Web site: www.casacolumbia.org

CASA is a private nonprofit organization that works to educate the public about the hazards of chemical dependency. The organization supports treatment as the best way to reduce chemical dependency. It produces publications describing the harmful effects of alcohol and drug addiction and effective ways to address the problem of substance abuse.

National Clearinghouse for Alcohol and Drug Information
11426-28 Rockville Pike, Suite 200
Rockville, MD 20052
(800) 729-6686
e-mail: webmaster@health.org
Web site: www.health.org

The clearinghouse distributes publications of the U.S. Department of Health and Human Services, the National Institute on Drug Abuse, and other federal agencies concerned with alcohol and drug abuse. Papers available on its Web site include "Tips for Teens: The Truth About Marijuana," "Marijuana: Facts Parents Need to Know," and "Wake Up to the Risks of Marijuana: A Guide for Parents."

National Organization for the Reform of Marijuana Laws (NORML)
1600 K St., Suite 501

Washington, DC 20006-2832
(202) 483-5500
fax: (202) 483-0057
e-mail: norml@norml.org
Web site: www.norml.org

Since its founding in 1970, NORML has provided a voice in the public policy debate for those Americans who oppose marijuana prohibition and favor an end to the practice of arresting marijuana smokers. A nonprofit public interest advocacy group, NORML represents the interests of the tens of millions of Americans who smoke marijuana.

The Partnership for a Drug-Free America
405 Lexington Ave., Suite 1601
New York, NY 10174
(212) 922-1560
fax: (212) 966-1570
Web site: www.drugfree.org

The Partnership for a Drug-Free America is a nonprofit coalition of communication, health, medical, and educational professionals working to reduce illicit drug use and help people live healthy, drug-free lives. Its research-based educational campaigns are disseminated on TV and radio and in print advertisements and over the Internet.

Patients Out of Time
Fish Pond Plantation,
1472 Fish Pond Rd.
Howardsville, VA 24562
(434) 263-4484
fax: (434) 263-6753
e-mail: patients@medicalcannabis.com
Web site: http://medicalcannabis.com

Patients Out of Time is a nonprofit advocacy organization that supports the rights of patients to have legal and safe access to the therapeutic use of cannabis. Its mission is to educate health-care professionals and the public about the medical benefits of cannabis.

Wo/Men's Alliance for Medical Marijuana (WAMM)
309 Cedar St., #39
Santa Cruz, CA 95060
e-mail: info@wamm.org
Web site: www.wamm.org

WAMM comprises seriously ill patients whose mission is to educate the general public regarding the medical benefits of marijuana. Its goal is to ensure that qualifying patients have access to safe and legal marijuana for the treatment of terminal and debilitating illnesses.

BIBLIOGRAPHY

Books

Alan Bock, *Waiting to Inhale: The Politics of Medical Marijuana.* Santa Ana, CA: Seven Locks, 2000.

Martin Booth, *Cannabis: A History.* New York: Thomas Dunne/St. Martin's, 2004.

Mitch Earleywine, *Understanding Marijuana: A New Look at the Scientific Evidence.* New York: Oxford University Press, 2002.

Rudolph Gerber, *Legalizing Marijuana: Drug Policy Reform and Prohibition Politics.* Westport, CT: Praeger, 2004.

Ted Gottfried, *Should Drugs Be Legalized?* Brookfield, CT: Twenty-First Century, 2000.

Lester Grinspoon and James Bakalar, *Marihuana: The Forbidden Medicine.* New Haven: Yale University Press, 1997.

William Hermes and Anne Galperin, *Marijuana: Its Effects on Mind and Body.* New York: Chelsea House, 1992.

Leslie L. Iversen, *The Science of Marijuana.* New York: Oxford University Press, 2000.

Alison Mack and Janet Joy, *Marijuana as Medicine? The Science Beyond the Controversy.* Washington, DC: National Academy Press, 2001.

Patrick Matthews, *Cannabis Culture: A Journey Through Disputed Territory.* London: Bloomsbury, 1999.

George McMahon, *Prescription Pot: A Leading Advocate's Heroic Battle to Legalize Medical Marijuana.* Far Hills, NJ: New Horizon, 2003.

Gabriel G. Nahas et al., eds., *Marihuana and Medicine.* Totowa, NJ: Humana Press, 1999.

Beverly Potter and Dan Joy, *The Healing Magic of Cannabis.* Berkeley, CA: Ronin, 1998.

Robert C. Randall, ed., *Cancer Treatment and Marijuana Therapy*. Washington, DC: Galen, 1990.

Christian Rätsch, *Marijuana Medicine: A World Tour of the Healing and Visionary Powers of Cannabis*. Rochester, VT: Healing Arts, 2001.

Ed Rosenthal, *Why Marijuana Should Be Legal*. 2nd ed. New York: Thunder's Mouth, 2003.

Paul Ruschmann, *Legalizing Marijuana*. Philadelphia: Chelsea House, 2004.

Lynn Etta Zimmer, *Marijuana Myths, Marijuana Facts: A Review of the Scientific Evidence*. New York: Lindesmith Center, 1997.

Periodicals

Jonathan Adler, "High Court Anxiety," *National Review*, December 1, 2004.

Alcoholism & Drug Abuse Weekly, "Doctors Reject Proposal Backing Medical Marijuana," vol. 13, no. 26, July 2, 2001.

Paul Armentano, "Marinol vs. Natural Cannabis: Pros, Cons and Options for Patients," NORML Foundation, August 11, 2005. www.norml.org.

Andrea Barthwell, "A Haze of Misinformation Clouds Issue of Medical Marijuana," *Los Angeles Times*, July 23, 2003.

Robert Charles, "Medical Pot Up in Smoke," *Washington Times*, June 9, 2005.

Alexander Cockburn, "The Right Not to Be in Pain: Using Marijuana for Pain Management," *Nation*, vol. 276, no. 4, February 3, 2003.

Sherwood Cole, "An Update on the Effects of Marijuana and Its Potential Medical Use: Forensic Focus," *Forensic Examiner*, vol. 14, no. 3, Fall 2005.

John Coleman, "Synthesized Cannabinoids as Medicine? Yes. Smoked Cannabis (Marijuana) as Medicine? No," *Drug Watch World News*, vol. 10, no. 1, March 2005.

Robert Dreyfuss and Tim Dickinson, "Bush's War on Pot," *Rolling Stone*, August 11, 2005.

Steve Ford, "Extra Pharmacopoeia," *British Medical Journal*, May 26, 2001.

Elisabeth Frater, "Medical Marijuana: The Smoldering Debate," *National Journal*, vol. 33, no. 11, March 17, 2001.

Dale H. Gieringer, "The Origins of California's 1913 Cannabis Law," *Journal of Contemporary Drug Problems*, vol. 26, no. 2, Summer 1999.

Nick Gillespie, "Medical Marijuana Madness," *Reason*, vol. 37, no. 4, August/September, 2005.

Lester Grinspoon, "The Medical Marijuana Problem," *Journal of Cognitive Liberties*, vol. 4, no. 2, 2003.

Harvard Health Letter, "Reefer Rx: Marijuana as Medicine," vol. 29, no. 11, September 2004.

Erin Hildebrandt, "Medical Marijuana," *Mothering*, May/June 2004.

Alain Joffe, W. Samuel Yancy, et al., "Legalization of Marijuana: Potential Impact on Youth," *Pediatrics*, vol. 113, no. 6, June 2004.

Brigid Kane, "Medical Marijuana: The Continuing Story," *Annals of Internal Medicine*, vol. 134, no. 12, June 19, 2001.

Richard Lowry, "Weed Whackers," *National Review*, August 20, 2001.

Apoorva Mandavilli, "Marijuana Researchers Reach for a Pot of Gold," *Nature Medicine*, vol. 9, no. 10, October 2003.

Billy Martin, "Medical Marijuana: Moving Beyond the Smoke," *Lancet*, vol. 360, no. 9326, July 6, 2002.

Robert McCord, "Legal Pot Is Bad Medicine," *Arkansas Times*, vol. 29, no. 27, February 1, 2003.

Ken Picard, "Smoke and Mirrors? Searching for Clarity on the Medical Marijuana Debate," *Seven Days*, vol. 9, no. 35, April 2004.

Sheldon Richman, "Medical Marijuana Is Not a Libertarian Cause," *Freedom Daily*, March 2005.

Richard H. Schwartz, "Marijuana: A Decade and a Half Later, Still a Crude Drug with Underappreciated Toxicity," *Pediatrics*, vol. 109, no. 2, February 2002.

Thomas Sowell, "Thomas Is Right About Commerce Clause," *Human Events*, vol. 61, no. 21, June 20, 2005.

Norm Stamper, "Let Those Dopers Be," *Los Angeles Times*, October 16, 2005.

Joel Stein, "The New Politics of Pot: Can It Go Legit?" *Time*, November 4, 2002.

Taylor Stuart, "Medical Marijuana and the Folly of the Drug War," *National Journal*, vol. 33, no. 20, May 19, 2001.

Chuck Thomas and Bruce Mirken, "Effective Arguments for Medical Marijuana Advocates," Marijuana Policy Project, July 2003. www.mpp.org/mmjargue.html.

Dean Wingerchuk, "Cannabis for Medical Purposes: Cultivating Science, Weeding Out the Fiction," *Lancet*, vol. 364, July 24, 2004.

Stephen Young, "Should This Woman Be Arrested?" *Chicago Reader*, vol. 34, no. 20, February 11, 2005.

INDEX

PICTURE CREDITS

Cover, © Joao Luiz Bulcao/CORBIS
Associated Press, AP, 10, 19, 20, 27, 31, 36, 42, 63, 73, 82
© Jeff Albertson/CORBIS, 69
© Joao Luiz Bulcao/CORBIS, 28
© Henry Diltz/CORBIS, 76
© Owen Franken/CORBIS, 51
© Scott Huston/CORBIS, 9
© Alleruzzo Maya/CORBIS, 54
© Jeffrey L. Rotman/CORBIS, 85
© Erik P./zefa/CORBIS, 9
Getty Images, 80
Lou Dematteis/Reuters/Landov, 25
Terry Schmidt/UPI/Landov, 48

ABOUT THE EDITOR

Elaine Minamide has written for numerous newspapers and magazines. She currently teaches English part-time at Palomar Community College in San Marcos, California.

EAU CLAIRE DISTRICT LIBRARY